ADDISON WESLEY LONGMAN HISTORY IN DEPTH SERIES

CAUSES OF THE SECOND WORLD WAR

Alan Monger
Series editor: Christopher Culpin

LONGMAN

CONTENTS

PART ONE

INTRODUCTION

On 11 November 1918, the fighting in the most widespread and destructive conflict in the history of the world ended. Politicians, people and soldiers were determined that such a disaster should never happen again. Yet, just over 20 years later, most of the main protagonists were at war again, mostly on the same sides as in 1914. This book attempts to explain how it happened.

The peace talks began in Paris on 18 January 1919. The Peace of Paris was mostly written by a 'Council of Ten' – two representatives from each of the five main Allied Powers (Britain, France, the USA, Italy and Japan). When there were difficult problems, however, the 'Big Three' (Wilson, Lloyd George and Clemenceau) settled them. Each brought his personal experiences, philosophy and prejudices to bear on the task and each was subject to domestic political pressures (see Picture Gallery on page 13).

As you look through the outline of events, think about the following questions:
- **What were the causes of the Second World War?**
- **How far were worsening international relations in the 1930s caused by the Great Depression?**
- **To what extent was the Second World War due to failures in international diplomacy between the wars?**
- **Why, in spite of the widespread revulsion after the First World War, did it prove impossible to achieve world disarmament?**
- **Did Hitler really intend to start the Second World War?**
- **What events led up to the Second World War?**
- **When did the Second World War become inevitable?**

Political, diplomatic and economic events

1918 (Nov.)	Armistice ends the Great War
1919–20	Negotiation of the Peace of Paris (including Treaty of Versailles)
1921	Reparations set at 132 billion gold marks
1922	Treaty of Rapallo between Germany and the USSR. Mussolini comes to power in Italy
1923	France and Belgium occupy the Ruhr
1924	Dawes Plan reschedules Germany's debts
1925	Locarno Pact signed by Britain, France, Italy and Germany
1926	Germany admitted to League of Nations
1928	Stalin emerges as winner of power struggle in USSR
1929 (Oct.)	The Wall Street Crash on US stock market
1929–33	Worst years of the Great Depression
1930	Nazi Party's success in German Reichstag elections
1931–2	Japanese invasion of Manchuria
1933 (Jan.)	Hitler becomes Chancellor of Germany
1934	First German attempt to gain control of Austria
1935	Saar district votes to return to German rule
1935 (June)	Stresa Front agreement between Britain, France and Italy
1935–6	Abyssinian Crisis: Italian invasion
1936 (March)	German reoccupation of the Rhineland
1936	Spanish Civil War
	Italo–German Pact – formation of 'the Axis'. German–Japanese Anti-Comintern Pact (anti-Russian)
1938 (March)	German invasion of Austria
(Sept.)	Munich Agreement: Czechoslovakia cedes Sudetenland to Germany
1939 (March)	German invasion of Czechoslovakia
	Pact of Steel between Mussolini and Hitler
(Aug.)	Nazi-Soviet Non-Aggression Pact
(Sept.)	German invasion of Poland. Britain and France declare war on Germany
1941	Japanese attack American fleet at Pearl Harbor. War begins in the Pacific.

1919–20: the peace treaties

Germany had sued for peace in November 1918 on the basis of President Wilson's 'Fourteen Points'. These *did* form the framework of the discussions but the Germans were not allowed to take part in the talks and were dismayed at the Treaty of Versailles in June 1919. It consisted of the following terms:

▲ *Germany's frontiers in Europe*: Germany lost Alsace and Lorraine which were returned to France. It also lost territory to Belgium, Denmark and Poland and was forbidden to unite with Austria. The west bank of the Rhine was 'demilitarised' and occupied by Allied troops.

▲ *Germany's colonial empire*: All of Germany's overseas colonies and trading concessions were taken from it by America, Japan, Britain or Dominions of the British Empire.

▲ *Armed forces*: The German navy was to be handed over to Britain, its army was to be reduced to a fraction of its former size and it was forbidden to begin to develop an air force.

The German people considered that each of these went too far and together they made up an unfair and unworkable set of demands.

Other peace treaties were made with the other defeated powers at other ex-palaces of the former Kings of France: the Treaty of St Germain with Austria (1919); the Treaty of Neuilly with Bulgaria (1919); the Treaty of Trianon with Hungary (1920); and the Treaty of Sèvres with Turkey (1920) – though the latter had to be renegotiated at Lausanne in 1923 when some of its clauses proved unsatisfactory.

The Peace of Paris included the creation of the League of Nations. As President Wilson's pet project, it was the first item settled and once he had achieved it, he lost interest in much that followed. Its first task was to supervise the carrying out of the 'Mandates', or special responsibilities, given to the victors to govern and guide the colonies taken from Germany and the non-Turkish territories taken from the Turkish Empire.

1920–24: the new Europe begins to settle down

Once the treaties had been made, there was a powerful desire in most west European countries except Germany to make them work. There were, inevitably, teething problems. When reparations were set in April 1921 at 132 milliard (billion) gold marks, there was an explosion of outrage and disbelief in Germany. In July 1922 the German government requested a three-year moratorium (delay) on the payments because of mounting inflation. International talks produced no agreement, so French and Belgian forces occupied the German industrial area of the Ruhr in 1923 to try to extract payment by force. This worsened the economic situation in both countries, and France eventually accepted an Anglo-American offer to attempt to work out a solution. The Dawes Plan (1924) tried to work out a more realistic schedule of payments and gave Germany economic advice. This was the end of the attempt to maintain the Versailles Treaty by force and the start of its gradual revision.

1925–29: the Locarno honeymoon period

During 'the Locarno honeymoon', it seemed that a revised version of the Treaty of Versailles might work. Gustav Stresemann – first as Chancellor and then as Foreign Minister of the Weimar Republic – began a policy of fulfilment of Germany's treaty obligations. Mussolini, after turning Italy into a one-party fascist dictatorship in 1925, seemed to be settling down to run his foreign affairs along fairly traditional lines. Western countries were beginning to trade with Russia again. This was partly due to domestic economic pressure – in the difficult postwar economic circumstances no country could afford to ignore a potentially huge market for long – and partly due to the fact that it was realised that the continuing political and economic isolation of both Germany and the USSR was beginning to drive them into each other's arms, as shown by the Treaty of Rapallo of 1922.

In this new atmosphere of ***détente***, the treaties made at Locarno in October 1925 looked as though they might be the final revision of

Versailles as far as western Europe was concerned. Delegates from Britain, France, Germany, Italy, Belgium, Poland and Czechoslovakia promised to uphold the terms of the Treaty of Versailles, in western Europe.

KEY TERM

Détente is a French word which means a relaxation after a period of strained relations between countries. It was used often during the 'Locarno honeymoon' period to express the wish, apparently on the part of all the west European powers, to establish a less tense atmosphere in European affairs.

The Pact started a brief period of attempts at international cooperation in place of confrontation. Locarno was the first time that the Germans were treated as equals at an international gathering since the end of the First World War.

The treaties were not received with universal enthusiasm. German nationalists complained that once again the Weimar government had accepted the humiliating terms of the Versailles Treaty. Those in France who hoped for a revival of the prewar alliance with Britain were also disappointed. Nevertheless, for a few years everything seemed to be moving in the right direction. Germany was admitted to the League of Nations in 1926, making the latter no longer just a 'league of victors'. In the late 1920s, the League was at the peak of its popularity and prestige. This diplomatic progress was supported by economic improvement: industrial production increased in almost all European countries in the late 1920s. Trade between Germany and France grew particularly rapidly. West European currencies stabilised again.

There were still potential problems, however. The Locarno Pact had fixed Germany's western frontiers more firmly than its eastern ones. No detailed arrangements were made to enforce its provisions. The Dawes Plan relied heavily on American loans to Germany. The League of Nations remained untried against a powerful, determined enemy.

1929–33: the worst years of the Great Depression

By the end of the 1920s economic problems were re-emerging in Europe. The Great Depression was triggered off not by European problems, however, but by an event in the USA. In October 1929 there occurred the 'Wall Street Crash'. In less than three years, the value of the shares in the American stock market fell from 89 to 15 billion dollars.

Although the USA had turned its back on European politics after the First World War, American banks had not withdrawn their investments in Europe. Once the Dawes Plan was working, Britain, France and Italy had been using German reparations payments to repay their debts to America. Germany had borrowed much of that money from American investors. Following the Wall Street Crash, a lot of this money was withdrawn from Europe by hard-up Americans. American imports from Europe dropped sharply and suddenly. The American financial and economic crises were thus exported rapidly to Europe.

The Great Depression was at its worst from 1929 to 1933 but many countries only began to recover in the late 1930s. It was so bad because there were so many contributory factors and because traditional economic policies (raising taxes and cutting government spending) used by most governments actually made things worse. Over-production of basic foods, such as wheat in the USA and the USSR, hit other agrarian-based economies hard. The shrinkage of international trade hit industrialised trading nations like Britain hard, too. The industrial recession this caused reduced the demand for raw materials from primary producers. As prices fell, so did company profits and the demand for services. There were runs on banks in many countries, as people withdrew their savings. The collapse of the international system of credit, which allowed trade to run smoothly, slowed business. When governments devalued their currencies, this made trade even more uncertain.

All these factors led to political instability. Even in Britain – the most stable of all European countries – there was a rise in support for extreme political groups. In France and Germany it became increasingly difficult for moderate governments to take the tough decisions necessary to deal with the economic crisis. The Communists on the left and Fascists on the right sought to take advantage of the situation. In Germany, when the Weimar governments used deflationary methods, unemployment soared. The popularity of the Nazi Party grew and it made impressive advances in the Reichstag (German Parliament) elections of September 1930. This alarmed American investors, and the withdrawal of American loans from Germany accelerated. In Japan the slump strengthened the hand of those who argued that expansion, into China, was the only way for Japan to defeat the crisis. Benito Mussolini, less bound by traditional economic theory, took state action to soften the impact of the slump but even Italy was hit by the shrinkage in world trade and living standards fell. Only the USSR, now well into Stalin's Five-Year Plans, felt little impact.

At this point, all the dictators who played leading parts in causing the Second World War were in power. There are profiles of Mussolini, Hitler and Stalin in the Picture Gallery (see pages 14–15).

1933–6: the political turning-point

During these years, as economies slowly recovered from the Great Depression, international tensions also began to revive. Even before this, the first fighting had broken out in the Far East. Between September 1931 and February 1932 Japan had seized the Chinese province of Manchuria, claiming to be protecting its commercial interests there in the face of a breakdown of Chinese authority. This was just the sort of action which the League of Nations had been set up to prevent: an attack on one member state by another. The League's Commission of Inquiry rejected Japan's claims and recommended the creation of an autonomous Chinese state of Manchuria. Japan rejected the Commission's findings and withdrew from the League which took no further action. It was unable to do much because the only other countries with sufficient military presence in the area – the USSR and the USA – did not belong to the League either. This was a crucial moment in the history of the League: it had failed its first serious test. Yet China was a backward country – far away from Europe where most of the Great Powers lay – and some politicians still clung to the belief that when it had to deal with problems closer to home the League would do better.

In Europe, Hitler was consolidating his power in Germany and making his first moves in foreign affairs. Between 1933 and 1935 he began to rearm Germany. In 1935 a plebiscite in the Saar voted overwhelmingly in favour of returning to German rule. Hitler was able to claim this as a Nazi victory. In March 1936 with the rest of Europe preoccupied with the Abyssinian Crisis, he reoccupied the Rhineland. Mussolini had been growing frustrated with the lack of spectacular success in his foreign policy. He had also been trying to gain influence over Abyssinia by befriending and increasing trade with it. The dispute between Abyssinia and Italy began in December 1934. As both were members, the League was asked to arbitrate but Italy continued to prepare for a full-scale invasion.

While this was happening, Mussolini signed the Stresa Front agreement with Britain and France. The powers pledged their support for the Locarno Pact, condemned Hitler's unilateral breach of it in going ahead with German rearmament, and warned him against attempting to seize Austria. Now Britain and France were caught in a dilemma. They needed Mussolini as a brake on Hitler but the other members of the League were watching them. If the League failed to protect a weaker country against an aggressive power again, they would conclude that it was useless. The democracies tried to find a compromise which gave Mussolini most of what he wanted while leaving the Emperor of Ethiopia on his throne. Mussolini nevertheless quit the League and launched his invasion in October 1935. The vast majority of League members voted for sanctions. Britain and France now claimed to support them, while ensuring that they failed, and in May 1936 the Italian conquest was completed. Britain and France had managed to achieve the worst of both worlds. They and the League were now utterly discredited as upholders of international law. Mussolini was not grateful to them and they could not rely on him as an ally against Hitler.

Although today **'appeasement'** is a derogatory word, it was popular at the time, at least until after Munich. After the discrediting of the League of Nations, there seemed to be no alternative. Systems of alliance and deterrence were still discredited in the eyes of those who believed that they had contributed to the outbreak of war in 1914. Those who opposed appeasement, like Winston Churchill, were very much the exception at the time.

KEY TERM

Appeasement was defined in 1925 by Austen Chamberlain as 'the removal of potential sources of friction and conflict through negotiation and the promotion of peaceful change'. Neville Chamberlain took it up with enthusiasm in 1937, talking about 'a general scheme of appeasement' as the solution to the growing tension in Europe. He believed that the powers who were dissatisfied with Versailles, especially Germany, had legitimate grievances and that these should be rectified. He believed that Germany had a right to unite with Austria, to the Sudetenland and to regain Danzig. He also believed that if these injustices were righted then Germany would cease to be aggressive.

1936–9: the approach of the Second World War

The outbreak of the Spanish Civil War in July 1936 exposed the dilemma facing the democracies. It was a struggle between the left-wing Republican government and the rebel Fascist forces led by General Franco. It was no direct concern of any other country in Europe and yet both of the Fascist dictators sent help to Franco. The two democracies – ill-prepared for armed conflict and, in Britain's case, with some government sympathy for Franco – made the excuse that it was an internal conflict and therefore neutrality was the proper policy to follow. (Thus, with valuable foreign support, Franco won.)

Following the Spanish Civil War, Hitler and Mussolini moved closer together. In November 1936 they announced the 'Italo–German Pact' and declared that European affairs would henceforth revolve around the 'Axis' they had just formed. In 1937 Mussolini joined the Anti-Comintern Pact that Hitler had made with Japan (mainly directed against the USSR) in 1936. By now, a formation of dissatisfied, ambitious, aggressive Powers who had all left the League of Nations was firmly established. Also, Mussolini no longer stood between Hitler and his desire to unite Austria and Germany. Hitler found an excuse to invade Austria in March 1938. As well as a great propaganda coup, this was the first success which added significantly to Germany's economic and military strength.

Hitler next turned his attention to Czechoslovakia. Preparations for the invasion began in May 1938 and by September he was making public threats of war and demanding self-determination for the Sudeten Germans. At this point, Neville Chamberlain flew to Germany to mediate. Certain that this was Hitler's last major grievance, Chamberlain persuaded the French government to support him in making the Czechs cede the Sudetenland to Germany without a fight. The Munich Pact left Czechoslovakia defenceless against a future German attack but did not satisfy Hitler. In the spring of 1939, he used the excuse of continued unrest in Czechoslovakia to invade the country. He absorbed the Czech part (Bohemia) into his Third Reich and set up a puppet regime in Slovakia.

Britain and France now recognised that appeasement had failed. They promised support to Poland, Romania and Greece in the hope of warning Hitler off. But Hitler had made his own diplomatic preparations which he hoped would show Britain and France that their intervention would be pointless: he had made alliances with the Baltic countries (Latvia, Estonia and Lithuania), Italy (the 'Pact of Steel') and, in August 1939, the Nazi–Soviet Non-Aggression Pact. With Poland now surrounded by hostile or unfriendly neutral powers, how could Britain and France hope to save it? Hitler was right to think that they could not save Poland but wrong to believe they would do nothing. When he invaded Poland on 1 September 1939, Britain and France declared war on him two days later. The Second World War in Europe had begun.

On the other side of the world, Japan had been growing increasingly isolated during the late 1930s. Despairing of ever getting widespread acceptance of its expansion into China and the Pacific, Japan had concluded that war with the other imperial powers in the area was inevitable. Japan decided that its best course was to make a pre-emptive strike against the main enemy force in the area and attacked the American fleet at Pearl Harbor in 1941. Thus the conflict became a global one.

Woodrow Wilson (President of the USA)
1856–1924

Born the son of a Presbyterian minister, Wilson was no career politician, having been a professor at Princeton before entering politics. In 1910 he became Governor of New Jersey and in 1912 was elected President so, when war broke out in 1914, he had just four years' experience in government. Also, he had far less personal involvement in the war than either **Clemenceau** or **Lloyd George**. With his religious upbringing and academic career, it is not surprising that Wilson saw US entry to the war in 1917 as an opportunity to achieve a fairer system of international relations, democracy and the right to self-determination. In January 1918 he set out 'Fourteen Points' as a framework for peace talks.

Georges Clemenceau (Premier of France)
1841–1929

Although 76, with a long stormy career behind him, Clemenceau proved he was still a tough, dynamic politician in 1918. Known as 'The Tiger' for his political ferocity, historians disagree about Clemenceau's approach to the peace settlement with Germany. Richard Watt in *The Kings Depart* (1968) called Clemenceau a 'Germanophobe'. He had good reason to be: in 1871 he had helped to defend Paris in the war in which France had lost Alsace-Lorraine to Germany. More recent historians, however, while conceding that Clemenceau hated the Germans, stress that he was prepared to compromise if this would promote a lasting peace.

David Lloyd George (Prime Minister of Great Britain) *1863–1945*

In 1918 Lloyd George needed a peace that would satisfy the British electorate, protect his own political future and, at the same time, create a viable post-war Europe. He became Prime Minister in 1916 because the public felt that only he could make a real difference to the war effort. His scheming to obtain the post split the Liberal Party from which he was alienated. He only had a majority in the British Parliament as long as he could keep the support of the Conservatives.

Benito Mussolini *1883–1945* (led Italy 1922–43)

The first of the Second World War dictators to come to power, having only set up his Fascist Party in 1919. Mussolini acted cautiously at first but by 1924 had turned Italy into a fascist state. He removed all other political parties and as many other sources of potential opposition as he could, though he left the Catholic Church largely untouched. He tried to solve Italy's economic problems by various measures, including public works schemes, agricultural self-sufficiency and the promotion of prestige and military industries. He also tried to raise Italy's standing in the world. He did this at first by seeking revision of the Treaty of Versailles but when this yielded only limited gains he began to think in terms of military expansion. Mussolini was killed by partisan bullet in April 1945.

Joseph Stalin *1879–1953* (ruled the USSR from c1928 to 1953)

When Lenin died in 1924, Stalin (born Josef Vissarionovich Dzhugashvili) was already one of the top politicians in the USSR. His victory in the ensuing power struggle (1924–8) was due in part to the fact that his policy of building 'Socialism in one country' was both more practicable and more appealing to a war-weary Russian people than his opponents' ideas. It involved the USSR turning away from world revolution and making itself wealthy and strong enough to survive in a world dominated by hostile capitalist powers. The series of Five Year Plans, from 1928 to 1940, were designed to transform the USSR from a backward agrarian-based economy into an advanced industrial country. This would enable it to hold its head high among the other great powers and to produce its own sophisticated weaponry with which to defend itself from them, if necessary. It is also one of the reasons why the Soviet Union played a fairly low-key role in inter-war international affairs: it saw itself as working desperately to catch up with the West before it was too late. Stalin died in April 1953 of a brain haemorrhage.

Adolf Hitler *1889–1945* (led Germany from 1933 to 1945)

In 1918 Hitler joined the German Workers' Party. By 1921, he had become its Führer (leader) and changed its name to the National Socialist Party. It became more violent, trying unsuccessfully to seize power in Bavaria in 1923. Hitler spent the rest of the 1920s consolidating his position within the party and when the Great Depression struck he was in a good position to take advantage of the Weimar politicians' inability to deal decisively with the situation. He eventually achieved the Chancellorship in January 1933 and rapidly turned Germany into a one-party state, drawing the reins of power into his own hands. In foreign affairs, he followed the twin policy of strengthening the armed forces and working to undo the clauses of Versailles which Germans regarded as harsh. Hitler reputedly committed suicide in a bunker in April 1945.

Neville Chamberlain *1869–1940*

Half-brother of Austen Chamberlain (British Foreign Secretary 1924–9), Neville had a successful business career before entering Parliament in 1918. He had little experience in foreign affairs before he became Prime Minister in May 1937. In spite of this, he took personal responsibility for his government's policies towards Hitler's Germany in the crucial two and a half years before the outbreak of the Second World War, believing that much could be achieved through personal meetings and discussion between Heads of Governments. Neville Chamberlain resigned as Prime Minister in May 1940 (Winston Churchill formed an all-party Coalition Government) and died six months later.

PART TWO

CHAPTER ONE

THE PEACE OF PARIS

Objectives

◢ To look at the scale and complexity of the problems faced by the peacemakers at Paris in 1919

◢ To show what went wrong during the negotiation of the 1919 Peace of Paris

◢ To decide if the Peace of Paris was a cause of the Second World War.

The Peace of Paris of 1919 has a poor reputation among historians, often being compared unfavourably with the Peace of Vienna which ended the Napoleonic Wars in 1815. Using this comparison may help to clarify the problems faced by the 1919 peacemakers: the Napoleonic Wars were the only previous conflict in modern times to approach the First World War in terms of devastation. The economies of the countries involved found it just as hard to readjust to peace as they did after the 1914–18 war. Feelings ran just as high in both wars. Yet, it seems, the 1815 settlement was moderate and brought peace to Europe for almost a century. By contrast, the Peace of Paris has been criticised for being too harsh, too lenient, too cynical, too impractical, too greedy and containing inconsistent and unrealistic decisions. It has also been identified by many as a cause of the Second World War.

The 1919 Peace of Paris was criticised at the time by cartoonists (see Figure 1), political commentators and politicians (see the sources below).

◢ Sources

… this treaty ignores the economic solidarity of Europe, and by aiming at the destruction of the economic life of Germany it threatens the health and prosperity of the Allies themselves. [It] … leaves Europe more unsettled than it found it.

John Maynard Keynes, the famous economist, in his book **The Economic Consequences of the Peace** *(1920)*

PEACE AND FUTURE CANNON FODDER

The Tiger: "Curious! I seem to hear a child weeping!"

Figure 1 British cartoon, published in *The Daily Herald*, May 1919. On the right the leaders of Britain, Italy, France and the USA are leaving Versailles. They can hear a child crying and are puzzled about where the weeping is coming from. The caption reads *The Tiger* (Clemenceau, the French Prime Minister): *"Curious! I seem to hear a child weeping!"*

I cannot think of any greater cause of future war than that the German people should be surrounded by a number of small states, each containing large masses of Germans demanding union with their native land. These proposals in my judgement must lead sooner or later to a new war in Eastern Europe.

David Lloyd George, British Prime Minister at the time of the Peace of Paris and one of its leading creators (1920)

What use could be made of the Treaty of Versailles! Each point of that Treaty could be branded in the minds and hearts of the German people until 60 million men and women are burning with rage and shame; and a torrent of fire bursts forth, and a will of steel is forged from it, with the common cry: We will have arms again!

*Adolf Hitler, **Mein Kampf** (1924)*

Later, in the 1920s and early 1930s, many in Britain shared the German feeling that the settlement had been too harsh on them. Yet the experience of the First World War was so dreadful that most ordinary people and politicians were determined that such a conflict should never happen again. In this book we will attempt to show what went wrong. Part of the answer lies in the scale and complexity of the problems facing the peacemakers.

Scale and complexity of the problems

There were huge differences between the problems faced by the peacemakers at Paris in 1919 and those of 1815:

1 New states for old

In 1815 the Russian and Habsburg **Empires** were on the winning side. Peace involved the restoration of those empires to their former size and power. By 1918 the Russian Empire had already been swept away, the Kaiser had abdicated to make it possible for Germany to make peace and the Habsburg Empire rapidly dissolved itself as its ex-provinces tried to avoid sharing the blame and the cost of the war. Three empires – two of them long-established, multinational states – had suddenly disintegrated: what would replace them? Compare the two maps of Europe (Figures 2 and 3 on pages 19 and 20). Notice how much less

Figure 2 Map of Europe in 1914

cluttered the prewar map of Europe looks than the postwar map with all the new nation-states.

KEY TERM

Empire: a state built up and controlled by a dominant nation (*e.g.* the Russian Empire) or ruling family (*e.g.* the Habsburgs in Austria). Its minority peoples together could outnumber the ruling nation (*e.g.* in 1907 the Russian Empire's population was only 45 per cent Russian). During the nineteenth century, these multi-nation states had been threatened by the rise of nationalism and the First World War was merely one stage in this struggle.

Figure 3 Map of Europe in 1924, after the Peace Treaties

2 Disputed territories

As well as questions of new regimes, the future of many other pieces of territory also had to be decided. These included lands that Germany had taken from Russia in the Treaty of Brest-Litovsk in March 1918. It could not be allowed to keep them but the Allies didn't want to hand them back to the new Communist regime in the USSR either. Also, although Germany had surrendered, its army still occupied a lot of territory in northern France and Belgium. This clearly had to be returned to France, but could it be safely assumed that the people of Alsace and Lorraine, taken from France by Germany nearly 50 years earlier, still wanted to return to French rule?

3 Public opinion

In 1919 the expectations of ordinary men and women had to be considered, whereas in 1815 *no* consideration was given to public opinion because it did not exist. Politics and literacy were still largely confined to the upper classes in those countries that had defeated France. The mass media, which both form and inform public opinion in this century, had yet to develop. In the 1914–18 War, however, far more of each country's population had fought, suffered, died, or worked in the war industries than ever before. In Britain, millions of young men had been pressured, coaxed and flattered into joining the armed forces. They had been told that they were fighting a war to save civilisation. French civilians in the war zones had seen their farms, homes, factories, mines and towns turned into something that resembled the surface of the moon and was about as fertile or productive. The British and French people wanted revenge, compensation and the better world they had been promised. American investors who had lent money, and businessmen who had sold goods on credit in Europe, watched anxiously to see whether the settlement would enable their debtors to pay up. All this meant that the negotiators had to consider not only what kind of clauses might work but also what their people would accept.

4 Ambitious newcomers

In 1815, after the Napoleonic Wars, there was only one power of any Europe-wide importance on the winning side which was not already regarded as one of the Great Powers: the rising north German state of Prussia. Prussia *was* rewarded with land but the three Great Powers took care to ensure that the gains did not turn Prussia into a more compact and cohesive state which could have become a threat to them. It took Prussia more than another 50 years to unite Germany.

Yet again, in 1919 the situation was more complex. There were now three victorious and ambitious countries, apart from the existing Great Powers: Italy, Japan and Serbia (or Yugoslavia as the new enlarged state was named). The problem was how to satisfy them without allowing them to become too powerful. France was nervous of Italian growth in the Mediterranean; Britain was worried by Japanese expansion in the Far East; Yugoslavia and Italy were rivals in the Adriatic. With Germany and Russia inevitably unhappy with any peace settlement, the Allies could not afford to leave Italy, Japan and Serbia unhappy too.

5 Germany down but not out

In 1815, after two centuries of expansion and a war in which it had fought most of the important countries in the world for over 20 years, France was close to exhaustion. It was also diplomatically isolated through having fought everyone. Alone, it no longer had the strength to threaten the peace of Europe.

Could the same be said of Germany in 1919? Its military commanders didn't regard their armies as defeated. Germany still retained most of its capacity to wage war. No German territory had been invaded and destroyed by enemy forces. The only way to reduce Germany's capacity to wage war in future would be deliberately to impose an extremely harsh peace upon it.

Again, unlike France in 1815, Germany was not the only defeated and diplomatically isolated Great Power at the end of the war: there was the Communist USSR too. The two had been bitter enemies in the war, but if both were treated harshly their common bitterness and isolation might drive them together. Lloyd George, for one, was keenly aware of this and worked to prevent it.

6 The size of the problem

This was greater in 1914–18. The Napoleonic Wars were essentially European – fought between European Powers although there was conflict at sea and in colonies overseas. In the First World War all this was still true but the involvement of the USA and Japan added further complexities to the peace talks as well as the fighting.

Conclusion

The peacemakers of 1919 faced a harder task than those of 1815 – and the 1815 settlement had not been an immediate success. There were riots and revolts in 1830 against some aspects of the settlement and the regimes it had restored. There were more serious revolutions in 1848. So, if the Peace of Paris didn't produce immediate and perfect peace in Europe and the rest of the world, we should not too easily assume that it was unworkable. It was bound to face some teething troubles because of the complexity of the task.

The negotiators and the negotiations

The problems faced by the Paris peacemakers were enormous and a settlement that satisfied everyone was impossible. Nevertheless, the peacemakers have been heavily criticised on the grounds that they did not achieve even the best settlement possible in the circumstances. They have been criticised for both individual and collective failings. Individually, they have been criticised: for a lack of political realism (US President Wilson); for being too anti-German (French Premier Clemenceau); and for trying to be all things to all people (British Prime Minister, Lloyd George). Collectively, they were criticised for making a peace that tried to give each of them some of their main objectives but was unworkable as a whole. Are these caricatures or reasonable representations of what happened?

1 The American standpoint

In January 1918 President Wilson put forward his 'Fourteen Points' as a framework for peace negotiations. Alongside commitments about specific territorial questions, he proposed several general principles, which are paraphrased here:

1   Peace agreements should be arrived at publicly and published in full.

2   Absolute freedom of navigation upon the seas.

3   A removal of as many restrictions on free trade as possible.

4   The reduction of each country's armed forces to the lowest point necessary to maintain internal peace.

5   All colonial claims should be settled freely and open-mindedly. The interests of the native peoples should have equal weight with those of the colonial powers.

9, 10, 12 and 13   These all included the idea, either explicitly or implicitly of '*self-determination*': disputed frontiers were to be decided along 'clearly recognisable lines of nationality'.

14   The creation of a 'general association of nations' to act as a sort of international peacekeeping body.

Key Term

Self-determination: Wilson believed that the First World War had been partly caused by the struggle between would-be nation-states and the old Empires. This problem would be solved if peoples were allowed to choose or 'determine' for themselves, in a 'plebiscite' (referendum) which state they would belong to in future.

These points aimed to remove what Wilson believed to be the main causes of the First World War. It is easy to criticise them: How could the first point ever be enforced? How could he hope to persuade Great Britain, the world's leading naval power, to accept point 2 which would mean surrendering one of her main advantages in warfare? How could the French ever be persuaded to disarm when they feared the Germans so much? Did such things as 'clearly recognisable lines of nationality' really exist?

But these were not the only problems with the 'Fourteen Points'. By the time he came to Europe for the peace talks, Wilson had given way to an objection from Lloyd George that point 2 was unacceptable because it made future use of a naval blockade impossible. Clemenceau had successfully insisted that Germany must pay compensation for all the damage it had caused during the war. Wilson himself insisted that the Kaiser must abdicate before negotiations began. Each of these would make the treaty seem less fair to German nationalists.

Wilson's position as the spokesman of US interests and the champion of world democracy was weakened by the American elections in which the opposition party had won control of both the Senate and the House of Representatives. Wilson would now have a tough fight to get Congress to accept any peace based on the 'Fourteen Points'. Thus any impractical idealism in his original proposals was bound to be watered down, regardless of any objections from the European leaders.

2 The European standpoint

As we have seen, the first approach made by Germany in October 1918 was to President Wilson. This left Clemenceau and Lloyd George waiting apprehensively while Wilson carried out preliminary talks. When it was revealed that if they would not agree to a peace based on the 'Fourteen Points', Wilson was prepared to negotiate a separate American peace with Germany, they realised that Wilson had trapped them. The alternative would be to fight on against Germany without American support. Even Clemenceau, the more anti-German of the two, had to admit that France was exhausted. Also, world opinion would see their refusal to accept a peace based on the 'Fourteen Points' as cynical and self-interested. The European leaders reluctantly gave way to Wilson on 5 November 1918. The Armistice followed on 11 November and peace talks began on 18 January 1919.

The Peace of Paris

The issues to be decided at Paris can be divided into those that were immediately pressing (frontiers settled and fighting to be ended); those that could wait a little (financial problems); and those concerning the long-term peace of Europe and the world and would take time to sort out.

Immediate problems

1 Germany's frontiers

To aid understanding of the territorial settlement mentioned in the rest of this chapter refer to Figure 3 on page 20. In the West (as set out in number 8 of Wilson's 'Fourteen Points'), the provinces of Alsace and

Lorraine were returned to France. Germany was more upset when France was given the coal production of the Saar district (under the League's administration) to compensate for the French mines which had been sabotaged by the retreating German armies. After 15 years, a plebiscite (referendum) would be held to decide whether the Saar would revert to German rule, opt for French rule or stay under League administration. Germany's only other losses on its western frontier were the little towns of Eupen, Malmedy and Moresnet which, with their surrounding countryside, were given to Belgium (point 7 of the 'Fourteen Points').

In the North, Germany's frontier with Denmark was revised after a plebiscite in Schleswig. The people of North Schleswig voted to return to Denmark, and their wishes were carried out.

In the East, Germany cannot have been surprised at losing land to the restored state of Poland as it was clearly implied in number 13 of Wilson's 'Fourteen Points'. In fact, it lost relatively little land actually occupied by Germans. A plebiscite, held in Upper Silesia in 1921, resulted in most of it remaining German. Nevertheless, Germans deeply resented the loss of the Vistula corridor, needed to give Poland access to the Baltic, but which physically separated East Prussia from the rest of Germany. Danzig, a port with a strong German population, was not merged into Poland, but became a free city – politically independent but available as a port for Poland on the Baltic coast.

2 German arms and defences

Germany was the only one of the Great Powers disarmed in the peace settlement. Its army and navy were cut to small fractions of their wartime size and it was forbidden to develop an air force at all. Part of the homeland – the Rhineland – was to be occupied by foreign troops for many years and permanently 'demilitarised' (*i.e.* Germany was not to build any defences there). These clauses of the Treaty of Versailles caused resentment and insecurity in Germany.

3 Germany's defeated allies

Separate treaties (though still part of the Peace of Paris) were made with Austria, Hungary, Bulgaria and Turkey. Like Germany, Austria, Hungary and Bulgaria were all disarmed and had to pay reparations though, even in proportion to their size, they were asked to contribute much less. As with Germany, whenever there was uncertainty about the future of a piece of territory, the decision went against them.

▲ *Austria: Treaty of St Germain (September 1919)*   Austria lost all the non-German territories of the Austrian half of the old prewar Empire. It was forbidden to make a political or economic union with Germany.

▲ *Hungary: Treaty of Trianon (June 1920)*   Hungary lost three-quarters of the territory of its half of the Empire. It was especially bitter about its losses to Czechoslovakia (Slovakia and Ruthenia).

▲ *Bulgaria: Treaty of Neuilly (November 1919)*   Bulgaria lost territory to Greece, Yugoslavia and Romania and along with it, its Aegean coastline.

▲ *Turkey: Treaties of Sèvres (August 1920) and Lausanne (July 1923)*   In the first of these treaties, in accordance with number 12 of Wilson's 'Fourteen Points', the Sultan gave up all claims to the non-Turkish territories of the old Turkish Empire. However, there was such a strong reaction, led by Mustapha Kemal, against the Treaty, that it was renegotiated in 1923. Turkey regained some land and the right to close the Straits between the Mediterranean and the Black Sea to hostile warships in wartime. This episode showed that it was possible for a determined leader to force a revision of the Peace.

4 The Russian Problem

If the Peace of Paris was going to work, its east European clauses had to be accepted by the new Russian government. The problem was that civil war was still raging in Russia between Red and White Russian armies. It was unclear what the new government was going to be. Thus the independence of the Baltic states (Latvia, Estonia and Lithuania) could not be fixed until 1920 when the Bolsheviks had won the civil war. The Poles hoped to annex part of the Ukraine but in the end needed French support to prevent the Russians advancing on Warsaw itself. The Treaty of Riga of March 1921 nonetheless gave Poland more of the Ukraine and Belorussia than the 'Big Three' had originally intended. About a third of the new Polish nation-state's population were not Poles at all, so it was on poor terms with most of its neighbours from the start, having quarrels about territory with Russia, Lithuania, Germany and Czechoslovakia.

5 Japan and the Far East

With Japan in possession of the German concessions in China and refusing to give them up, the peacemakers had to bow to the inevitable. The peace treaties gave official recognition to Japan's Chinese gains, arousing great nationalist resentment in China. China's refusal to sign the peace treaties was one of the main reasons for the USA's similar refusal. This part of the settlement was renegotiated in 1922 as part of the Washington Treaty agreements.

Slightly less urgent: reparations

Article 231 of the Treaty – the so-called '*War Guilt* Clause' – was included to ensure that Germany accepted responsibility for all the loss and damage suffered by Allied governments and their subjects. Although the leaders of the victorious powers had different ideas about how much Germany should or, more realistically, could be expected to pay, they all agreed on *reparations* in principle. The Germans had spent far less to lose the war than the Allies had to win it and all of them would now be in financial difficulties if they could not recover much of their increased national debts. Britain and France needed German reparations payments to hand over to the Americans to pay for the war materials they had bought on credit.

KEY TERM

Reparations and **War Guilt**   These ideas were thought up to satisfy the demands of the British and French that Germany must pay for the damage and suffering it had caused during the war. German payments were expected to enable the Allied governments to compensate those who had suffered loss as a result of the war. It was clearly not just Germany who had caused damage during the war, so in order to justify making it pay most of the reparations the concept of 'War Guilt' was also introduced into the Treaty. Germany had to sign a clause agreeing that it accepted the sole responsibility for starting the war and therefore, even if it didn't actually cause all the damage, it was to blame for it all.

Looking to the future

The territorial settlements, armament reductions and reparations that are described above had inevitably disappointed or angered many countries. How might they be made to keep the terms until they had grown accustomed to them?

1 The **League of Nations** was President Wilson's big idea and, he hoped, the answer to this question. Unfortunately, the victorious Allies had different ideas about the sort of organisation the League ought to be. Britain and the USA wanted a loose, flexible organisation; France wanted it to be a military alliance with power to intervene in both international disputes and the internal affairs of member-states if necessary. It was the Anglo-American model, with non-intervention in internal affairs, that was adopted.

The League's reliance on moral and economic pressure weakened it from the start. It could only apply economic or military sanctions under stringent conditions. It was further weakened by the decision not to allow defeated powers, such as Germany and the USSR, to join immediately and by the American failure to join.

2 The **disarmament** of Germany was justified in the treaty by claiming that it had been carried out as the prelude to a 'general limitation of the armaments of *all* nations' (one of Wilson's 'Fourteen Points'). Yet no formal machinery was created to compel Germany to carry out disarmament (although there would be Allied troops in Germany for 15 years). No clear time limits were set either for other countries to disarm or for Germany's externally imposed limitations to end.

3 **Freedom of navigation**: American annoyance at having its merchant shipping disrupted by both the British navy and German U-boats was behind this point. It was decided, however, to leave it until the League of Nations was up and running.

Like reparations, these untidy ends created a resentment that lingered at least as long as the problems remained unsolved.

4 **Colonial claims and the mandate system**: the territories concerned were Germany's *colonial* empire and the non-Turkish provinces of the Ottoman Empire. Wilson was determined that the wishes and interests of their native inhabitants should be a vital factor in the settlement and that they should not simply be annexed by whichever country had conquered them during the

war: Britain, its dominions, France or Japan. On the other hand, once a country has taken military possession of another, it may be impossible to dislodge them without being prepared to fight another war.

The concept of *mandates* was created to solve this dilemma. More advanced nations would look after these territories and help them to progress towards independence. It was recognised that, in the case of some of the less developed colonies, this would take many years. Mandates would be awarded and supervised by the League of Nations. It somewhat undermined the high moral tone of these provisions when, in May 1919, the League awarded mandates in all the former German colonies to precisely those countries which had invaded and conquered them in the war.

KEY TERM

A **colony** is an overseas territory belonging to the state whose subjects founded or conquered it. Most colonies at this time belonged to European states, who were thus said to have 'a **colonial** empire' (*e.g.* the British and French colonial empires). Colonies were useful to their owners as sources of cheap food and raw materials and as captive markets for manufactures.

Conclusions

The Peace of Paris was not a faultless peace settlement. There was no way – given all the circumstances, high emotions and unrealistic expectations that we have considered in this chapter – that it could have been. Nor was it even as good as it could have been but perhaps Wilson and his 'Fourteen Points' must take much of the blame for unrealistically raising expectations which, when disappointed, led many to despair of the Treaty.

1 Now that you have some idea what all the events on the timeline on page 4 mean, try this exercise to help fix them in your mind and to get some idea of the changes of mood during the period.

Take a sheet of A3 paper and turn it on its side. Put the timeline dates 1918 to 1941 down the left-hand side. Divide the sheet into three columns. Head the columns:

ENCOURAGING   NEUTRAL   WORRYING

In the 'Encouraging' column put all the events from 1918 to 1941 that you think might have encouraged people at the time to hope that things were gradually getting back to normal after the Great War. In the 'Worrying' column put all those things that you think might have made people at the time concerned that peace was not going to last. Put anything that you are not sure about in the 'Neutral' column.

Next, use the subheadings to divide your table into periods:

1919–20: the peace treaties
1920–4: the new Europe begins to settle down
1925–9: the Locarno honeymoon period
1929–33: the worst years of the Great Depression
1933–6: the political turning-point
1936–41: the approach of the Second World War

Finally, find some way of making the following different strands of international affairs stand out from each other (*e.g.* use highlighter pens or underline them in different colours):

Diplomatic events (those to do with agreements between nations, such as Pacts, Alliances and Treaties)
Economic events (those to do with finance, business and trade)
Military events (invasions, military occupation)
Political events (elections, change of ruler or government)

Now you can carry out some analysis of the period. Try to formulate some preliminary ideas about the following questions:

a When did events look most hopeful during the interwar period?

b Can you decide on a year which was the turning-point in international affairs (*i.e.* is there a clear moment when you could say that from this time on the Second World War was inevitable)?

c   When were the periods of greatest diplomatic activity and can you explain why this was?

d   By what date were the three great dictators (Hitler, Stalin and Mussolini) all in power and what relation does this bear to your answer to question **b**?

e   What part did diplomacy, economic, military and political affairs play in causing the Second World War?

f   How far do you think people at the time would have been aware of these trends?

Your answers to all of these questions can be only tentative but return to them at the end of each of chapters 2 to 5 in Part two and revise them in the light of your increasing knowledge and understanding.

2   Use this roleplay as an exercise to help you understand how the various countries felt about the Peace of Paris. Start by each taking on the role of one of the countries involved in the war and the peace talks. You need to prepare a limited amount of information – about a side of A4 each – in answer to these questions:

a   Why did you enter the war? (Was it an aggressive or defensive action from your point of view? Was it in support of an ally? What were your war aims?)

b   How did you do out of the peace settlement in terms of your war aims? (Do you feel safer/stronger now? How do you feel towards your allies – are you still on good terms with them or did they let you down? Which of your war aims did you achieve?)

c   How satisfied do you feel with the way things turned out? (Are you in favour of upholding the peace settlement or will you be seeking to alter it in your favour? Are you a 'status quo' or a 'revisionist' power?)

Hold an international conference organised by the League of Nations. Discuss possible revisions of the peace settlement. Can you come to a better solution than the Peace of Paris? If not, why not? If you can, try to identify the reasons why the original peacemakers couldn't.

(NB   This exercise will require some research beyond the pages of this book, especially for question **a**.)

CHAPTER TWO

ECONOMIC AFFAIRS AND THE CAUSES OF THE SECOND WORLD WAR

Objectives

◢ To look at the settlement of the economic clauses of the Treaty of Versailles

◢ To analyse the apparent economic recovery of 1924–9

◢ To agree what the Great Depression was and analyse its effects

◢ To study how Hitler's economic ideas contributed to the outbreak of war

◢ To ascertain whether worsening international relations in the 1930s were caused by the Great Depression.

The Great Depression (1929–33), which began right in the middle of the interwar period, has strong links with both world wars. It arose partly out of the economic legacy of the First World War and some of its effects were direct causes of the Second. First, the details of reparations payments had to be settled.

Settling the economic clauses of Versailles

The reparations settlement

It had cost the Allies, particularly France, far more to win the war than it had cost the Central Powers to lose it. Small wonder, then, that they pinned much of their hopes for rebuilding their economies on the payment of reparations by the only surviving Great Power among the losers, Germany.

The percentage of reparations awarded to each of the victorious Allies was settled at the Spa Conference in Belgium in July 1920:

France	52%
Britain and its Empire	22%
Italy	10%
Belgium	8%
Others	8%

The final sum was settled in April 1921. Germany had to pay 132 'milliard' (billion) gold marks or about £6,600 million at the rate of two milliard marks a year.

Arguments and attitudes

There has been argument about how fair and realistic the reparations settlement was. The Weimar government protested that the sum was impossibly high. It was supported by the British economist, John Maynard Keynes, who calculated that it was three times what Germany could afford. The French government insisted that it could and must be paid.

Modern historians remain divided but perhaps it doesn't really matter who is right in this argument. What did matter was that the Weimar government in Germany could not afford *politically* to pay reparations whether or not the German economy could have borne it. The regime was in its infancy, with no reserves of loyalty and few enthusiastic supporters. If they were to establish the new republic they could not meekly accept a policy to which the German people were so hostile. If they were to pay up at all, they would have to be forced to pay – and sufficient will to enforce reparations payments existed only in France. A further problem for France – and an indication of the lack of will to enforce it by Britain and America – was that there were no automatic enforcement clauses in the treaty.

The attempt to enforce reparations

When the scheme of reparations payments was announced in April 1921, it caused rage and disbelief in Germany. France had to threaten to occupy the Ruhr before the Weimar government grudgingly accepted it. In December 1921, however, Germany protested that rising inflation would make it impossible for it to meet the next instalment of payments.

By this time America had withdrawn from European political affairs and the British were becoming worried that reparations payments were hindering Germany's economic recovery, thus preventing a revival of its trade with Britain. Lloyd George met French and other European leaders at Cannes (January 1922) and Genoa (April–May 1922) and tried to get France to stop trying to enforce full reparations payments in exchange for a strong defensive alliance with Britain. Neither side was prepared to make enough concessions to reach agreement.

French politicians were not being stupidly stubborn in their refusal to agree to reductions. First, their people fervently believed that it was Germany's duty to pay for all the damage it had done to France and its people. Secondly, French politicians knew that Germany was potentially stronger than France – economically and demographically. They hoped to prevent that becoming reality by taking some of Germany's wealth and using it to top up France's. That was why France alone, of the Great Powers, was prepared to use force to collect reparations.

In July 1922 Germany asked for a three-year delay in its reparations payments. Britain tried to solve the crisis by suggesting that it would collect from its debtors, chiefly France, only what the USA demanded from it. This only annoyed the USA without satisfying France.

By January 1923 hope of a peaceful compromise was gone and the French Premier, Poincaré, with French public opinion outraged, had no choice but to occupy the Ruhr. The German population, encouraged by their government, resisted passively. The mark, as the Germans had said, rapidly lost all value. Faced with financial chaos the Weimar government had to back down and resume payments. France had won the battle over reparations, only to lose the peace. The American government, still heavily financially involved in Europe, took part in the London Reparations Conference of July–August 1924. Much of the Dawes Plan produced here was drawn up by American bankers. France had to evacuate the Ruhr without any significant gain. France learned from the Ruhr occupation that it was futile to try to enforce Versailles alone. France needed the support of Britain against Germany and it chose that, rather than act alone any longer.

The apparent economic recovery of 1924–9

In the Locarno Pact of 1925 the four main west European powers – Britain, France, Italy and Germany – agreed that the terms of the Treaty of Versailles relating to western Europe were now settled. It looked as though the territorial and political disputes were now over and Europe could look forward to a period of better international relations. There was hope that economic problems might also be coming to an end.

The Dawes Plan (1924)

The Dawes Plan, to reschedule reparations payments, began a more settled economic period. Produced by a sub-committee of the Reparations Committee, under its American chairman Charles G. Dawes, it did not reduce the overall amount that Germany was asked to pay. Instead, annual repayments were to restart at a low level and only regain their full level by 1929. This would reduce the proportion of national income that Germany was being asked to pay during the 1924–9 period by half. France was unhappy because there were still no clauses in the plan for forcing Germany to pay up if it again attempted to default on payments, but agreed to the Dawes Plan in order to avoid diplomatic isolation.

American loans to Germany

It did seem more likely that Germany would pay up this time because it was given substantial American loans to pay reparations and to rebuild the German economy. This started such a remarkable recovery that by 1929 Germany was again one of the world's leading industrial economies. To achieve this, however, Germany had borrowed four to five times as much from the USA as it paid in reparations.

Alongside the new reparations schedule, the USA had by 1926 scaled down its demands for repayment of its former allies' debts, though it was still demanding repayment in gold and dollars. This led to debtor countries having problems in obtaining the necessary hard currency.

Unsolved problems

By 1925, however, it looked to many as though Europe might be about to begin a new era of prosperity. It had regained 1913 levels in output of food, raw materials and manufactured goods. But this broadly favourable picture concealed many persistent problems:

1 Governments sought to **return to the Gold Standard** in an effort to stabilise their currencies and thus make the conditions of international trade more certain. This would only work, however, if the relationship between the price of gold and a particular currency was also right compared with other currencies. Unfortunately, this was not always the case. The British government, for instance, had tried for reasons of politics and prestige to restore the pound to its prewar gold value. This overvalued the pound compared to the

dollar and made it difficult for Britain's manufacturers to increase their exports as their goods were overpriced.

2 **Over-production of agricultural produce**, especially grain, caused problems for the less industrially advanced countries. Germany, for instance, could subsidise its farmers to protect them from competition from cheap food imports. For the new countries in south and eastern Europe (Poland, Yugoslavia, Romania and Czechoslovakia) this was an unaffordable luxury. They had had to borrow heavily to set up their governments and relied on their agriculture to produce goods to repay those debts. As they tried to do so by increasing grain exports so, in a glutted market, the price they could get for those exports fell.

3 **The economic recovery by 1925 was uneven**. It was general, not universal. As well as agriculture-based economies, some primary producers also did poorly as the chemical industries of the advanced countries found substitutes for items such as coal and natural nitrate deposits. After the immediate postwar boom (1919–21) caused by the need to replace damaged equipment such as railways and shipping, heavy industrial areas found it difficult to win orders.

Thus some industries, regions, social classes and even whole countries had little share in the economic revival. Unemployment (and social discontent and distress) meant a fragile recovery.

The German economy in trouble again

In 1928, as the date for full reparations payments grew closer, the German government again approached the Allied governments with an appeal for a downward revision. American bankers, hearing reports of lockouts in the Ruhr and bankruptcies among leading German businesses, were already worried that Germany would be unable to pay both reparations and the interest on the American loans it had borrowed since 1924. So, early in 1929, a committee, under the banker Young, prepared a 'final and definite settlement'. It reduced the overall sum to 40 milliard gold marks and gave Germany until 1988 (!) to pay. Payments would, as with the Dawes Plan, start low and gradually increase. Another American loan was given to kick the scheme off and the Reparations Agency was disbanded.

It was all too late. With the German economy already in severe difficulties, the Wall Street Crash of October 1929 killed off American loans to Germany and the Great Depression began.

The Great Depression

The Great Depression was a period – 1929 to 1933 – when world trade, industrial output and employment declined drastically (see Figures 4 and 5, page 40). It reduced the volume of world trade by about 70% and had a huge impact on the economies of all those countries much involved in that trade. For a long time, also, it seemed that whatever governments tried to do to combat the depression either made little difference or often made matters worse.

How did it begin?
The Great Depression began in the USA in the autumn of 1929. Shares on the American stock market were already over-valued as a result of speculation. Bumper harvests (especially wheat) that year led to a glut which, in turn, led to falling prices and reduced farmers' incomes. This crisis in America's rural economy contributed to a collapse of confidence about the future of all businesses in America: less money in farmers' pockets would mean a drop in orders for such things as farm machinery or consumer goods; unpaid bank loans and mortgages could lead to the collapse of banks, insurance companies and other financial institutions. So, many investors, who had seen the value of their shares in these companies rise impressively during the 1920s, decided that this was a good time to sell them. This started a period of share selling which began on 3 October and went into panic mode three weeks later as investors saw the value of their shares falling more rapidly. This was the 'Wall Street Crash' when many companies' shares lost so much of their value that they went broke.

How did it spread?
This economic and financial crisis was exported to the rest of the world when American banks and private investors began to call in their loans from abroad to avoid bankruptcy; and the price of wheat on the world market collapsed. Russia (trying to pay for rapid industrialisation in its Five Year Plans from 1928) didn't help wheat prices by increasing grain exports in an effort to maintain its income from foreign currency. All

countries who owed money to the USA were affected, including Britain, France and Germany. All wheat-producing countries, especially those in eastern Europe who needed to sell grain to pay interest on their national debts, were badly hit too. Once this number of economically important countries was in trouble, difficulties multiplied:

◢ There was a crisis in credit and banking *e.g.* in May 1931 the Credit Anstalt, Austria's leading bank, went bankrupt. It had a large financial stake in about two-thirds of all Austrian industry and, as part of the legacy of its prewar empire, in many other businesses in central Europe. This crisis shook economic confidence over much of central Europe, especially Germany.

◢ The shrinkage of international trade (see Figures 4 and 5).

◢ Heavy unemployment in industrialised countries: in 1932 British unemployment was 3 million and Germany (with a roughly comparable population) had twice that; in the USA, with a much larger population, there were 13 million unemployed.

◢ Falls in the prices of all commodities and the demand for services from lawyers and accountants to barbers.

The effects of the Great Depression

To assess how far the Great Depression contributed to the worsening of international relations which preceded the Second World War, we must look at how it affected the leading powers internally and their attitudes towards each other.

1 In **Britain**, the effects were both typical of those it had on other major industrial and commercial countries and, at the same time, less severe. *Economically*, the falling volume of world trade led to lower industrial demand and therefore production; in turn, these led to unemployment, falling government income from taxes and increased government spending, especially on the dole. *Politically*, the financial crisis led to the fall of the Labour government and its replacement by a coalition (very unusual in British peacetime politics) dominated by the Conservatives. The new government devalued the pound by about 30 per cent which, with sterling still being the most important international currency, upset many investors with assets in sterling and made international trade in the currency uncertain.

Figure 4 Web diagram showing contracting international trade, 1929–33 (Source: C. P. Kindleberger *The World in Depression, 1929–39* (1972))

Month	1929	1930	1931	1932	1933
1	2997.7	2738.9	1838.9	1206	992.4
2	2630.3	2454.6	1700.5	1186.7	944
3	2814.8	2563.9	1889.1	1230.4	1056.9
4	3039.1	2449.9	1796.4	1212.8	
5	2967.6	2447	1764.3	1150.5	
6	2791	2325.7	1732.3	1144.7	
7	2813.9	2189.5	1679.6	993.7	
8	2818.5	2137.7	1585.9	1004.6	
9	2773.9	2164.8	1572.1	1029.6	
10	2966.8	2300.8	1556.3	1090.4	
11	2888.8	2051.3	1470	1093.3	
12	2793.9	2095.9	1426.9	1121.2	

Figure 5 These figures are from January 1929 to March 1933; total imports of 75 countries, monthly values given in terms of millions of old US gold dollars. (Source: League of Nations, *Monthly Bulletin of Statistics*, February 1934)

The effects were less severe for Britain than for some of the newer European countries because it was able to turn to its empire. It introduced a system of Imperial Preference, encouraging trade between itself and its colonies by putting up customs duties on goods from outside the Empire. This system of *imperial self-sufficiency* – they bought British manufactures in return for Britain buying their food and raw materials – helped to maintain the volume of Britain's trade. This helped it to remain politically stable, at the price of increasing British isolation from European trade and affairs. In particular, it weakened Britain's economic links with eastern Europe by reducing its food imports from there and allowing Germany the opportunity to step in and increase both its trade and influence in the area.

2 **France**, with a different economy from Britain (strong agriculture as well as industry, less dependent on foreign trade), felt the effects of the Great Depression more slowly but for considerably longer. The French economy did not really begin to recover until about a year before the Second World War broke out.

Like Britain, France both followed traditional deflationary economic policies at home and tried to tie its economy more closely to its own large empire by a system of imperial preference. Unlike Britain, France struggled for far longer (until 1936) to keep the franc on the Gold Standard which hindered foreign trade by making its exports overpriced.

If the economic effects of the Depression lasted longer in France than Britain, the political effects were also more severe. Under the Third Republic (1871–1940), French governments were notoriously unstable and always found it difficult to carry through unpalatable reforms, especially financial ones. Both of these tendencies were exaggerated by the Depression. There were 11 ministries from 1932 to 1935 because spending cuts were repeatedly rejected by the National Assembly (the lower house of the French parliament). These and other political problems led to greater support for extremist parties, including Nazi sympathisers on the Right.

France's prolonged depression and economic policy of imperial preference weakened its influence with the 'Little Entente' allies in eastern Europe (see chapter 3 page 53). France's political weakness and divisions led Hitler to believe that it would probably be unable to mount strong opposition to German expansion in the late 1930s (see *Hossbach Protocol* in chapter 5).

3 Thus the Great Depression had greatly affected both the economies and politics of the two European liberal democracies. Both had reserves of political loyalty and colonial empires upon which to draw in these difficult times. The Weimar Republic in **Germany** was weaker in all these respects. Its political system was new and unloved and Germany had lost its colonial empire, such as it was, in the Versailles settlement. It was like the French Third Republic only in one unfortunate respect: the French and German republican constitutions, in an effort to create regimes that were as democratic as possible, both gave a greater share of power to their legislatures (elected law-making assemblies) than their governments. This made it more difficult for French and German governments to take tough and unpopular finan- cial measures to deal with the crisis. Add to all this the fact that the German economy was in trouble even before the Depression and you can see that Germany was likely to suffer more seriously from it than either Britain or France.

It did. Industrial production fell; there was a bank crisis in 1931; unem- ployment rose further and faster than in Britain and France – from 2.4 million in March 1930 to 6 million (or 30 per cent of the work- force) by May 1932. Like his British and French counterparts, Chancellor Heinrich Brüning's Coalition Government followed strict deflationary policies until it fell in May 1932. Haunted by the 1923 experience of hyperinflation, it dared not devalue the mark as Britain had done with sterling. This left German exports overpriced so that they fell even faster than the fall in world trade.

As the crisis continued, Hitler's insistence that he had the answer to these and other problems appealed increasingly to a people more used to charismatic leaders than the uninspiring Weimar politicians. As the Nazi Party grew, the nervousness of foreign investors increased and they withdrew more funds from the German economy, making life even more difficult for the Weimar politicians.

Ironically the German economy had begun to recover before Hitler came to power. The Lausanne Conference of June 1932 virtually ended reparations. The Chancellors who followed Brüning – Franz von Papen and Kurt von Schleicher – abandoned deflation and began cautiously to reflate the German economy by encouraging borrowing, increasing government spending and starting public works schemes (building new roads, *etc.*). By then it was too late – the chain of events that would bring Hitler to power had already begun and he was able to take the credit for the recovery. The Great Depression gave Hitler the opportunity to pose as the saviour of Germany. In the end, however, it was he who seized that chance with great skill and determination.

We have seen that the Great Depression hit the European democracies hard. Did those powers that were already governed by dictatorial regimes, with no political opposition to criticise them and with powerful propaganda machines behind them, cope any better?

4 **Italy** had been under Benito Mussolini's rule since 1922 and officially a one-party Fascist state since 1924. At that time, Mussolini had stated his wish for a period of 'work and calm' in a country that had been economically and psychologically drained by the First World War and then bitterly divided by the period of industrial unrest that followed until 1922. He could claim that he had been successful up to 1929 but the Fascist economy proved no better at coping with the Great Depression than others. The industries of northern Italy were badly hit and production fell by a third. As elsewhere, unemployment was high and, with maintaining the value of the lira a matter of Fascist pride, Italy's products were overpriced so that foreign trade shrank by two-thirds.

Mussolini responded by raising import duties, introducing licences to restrict the quantity of imports, restricting the exchange of foreign currency and introducing a policy of 'self-sufficiency'. Italy was far less well-placed for it, however, than Britain or France with their large, wealthy, colonial empires and the policy had limited success. In the end, the lira had to be devalued in 1936 by 41 per cent. The invasion of Abyssinia in 1935–6 was in part an attempt by Mussolini to take Italian minds off the failure of his economic policies. To that extent, it is another example of how the Great Depression's effects stretch out towards the Second World War.

5 By contrast, the **Union of Soviet Socialist Republics** (USSR) had launched the first of its expansionary Five Year Plans in 1928 just before the Great Depression struck. The Plans were not a response to the Depression but were motivated by Stalin's conviction that the capitalist powers would crush Russia as soon as a convenient opportunity presented itself unless it could make itself strong enough – economically, industrially, technologically and militarily – to ward them off. The USSR was virtually self-sufficient in raw materials and food and the only way in which it was much affected by the Great Depression was its need to import advanced western machinery and technological knowhow. It had planned to pay for this by exporting grain but the world grain surplus that existed for the whole of the 1930s made it more difficult for the USSR to raise the hard cash it needed to pay suspicious suppliers abroad. Apart from that, the main impact of the Great Depression on Russia was the concern caused by the increasing militarism of the right-wing movements in Germany and other East European states.

Conclusion

The Great Depression seemed to turn all countries' gaze inward upon their own problems, at a time when international relations needed a great deal of attention. Economic problems took priority over the maintenance of good relations and influence abroad. The Depression weakened the democracies internally as well as reducing their clout abroad – France and Weimar Germany especially, and perhaps crucially. It also made Mussolini anxious to find some way of distracting his people from their day-to-day hardships. The Anglo-French economic withdrawal from eastern Europe gave Hitler's Germany the opportunity in the late 1930s to expand its influence in the area he had marked out in *Mein Kampf* as the new **lebensraum** that Germany needed.

Hitler's economic ideas and the coming of war

Adolf Hitler, in power from January 1933, had radically different ideas about economics from the traditional politicians of the time. First, he believed that he could make economic ideas serve his political and military ambitions, instead of thinking of economic problems as constraints on his freedom to act, as most politicians did. Secondly, unlike the democracies who wished to avoid war at least partly because the First World War had landed them so deeply in debt, Hitler believed that war could be made to pay. Behind these beliefs lay the concepts of **autarky** and *lebensraum*.

KEY TERMS

The German word **autarky** stands for Hitler's belief that it was the duty of the government to provide the best conditions it could for the lives and development of its people. This included being as self-sufficient as possible in food, fuel and essential raw materials. For some time, Germany had relied heavily on imported food, fuel and raw materials which it had paid for by exporting manufactured goods. Hitler believed that this left Germany unhealthily dependent on good relations with both its customers and suppliers and exposed to the dangers of a crisis in world trade – like the Great Depression.

Germany, therefore, needed more land (**lebensraum** means literally 'room to live') so that its farmers could produce the necessary food. Hitler had decided, long before he came to power and before the Great Depression, that this *lebensraum* could be acquired by conquering lands to the east of Germany – Poland, Czechoslovakia and the Ukraine.

If Hitler had developed these ideas before it began, the Great Depression convinced him he was right. Britain and France, using their colonial empires to cushion themselves against its worst effects, were practising a kind of *autarky*. Germany was unable to pay for essential imports when the volume and value of its exports were falling.

Nevertheless, Hitler's first moves in economic policy did not at first sight seem at all unorthodox. He used Brüning's plans for a cautious reflation of the economy. Then he stepped into the vacuum left by the British and French withdrawal from trade with eastern Europe. Advantageous trade deals were made in 1934–5 with Hungary, Yugoslavia and Romania. He started a new policy of importing food and raw materials from neighbouring states which became increasingly dependent on trade with Germany. For Hitler, however, these trade deals carried the bonus that they would not be subject to sanctions or naval blockade in time of war. Hitler's new Economics Minister (from July 1934), Hjalmar Schacht, balanced Germany's foreign trade by a system of import licences and reciprocal arrangements with foreign countries – again especially favouring those nearby in south-eastern Europe.

By 1936, however, tension was growing between Schacht and Hitler, the real aim of whose economic policies was to put the German economy on a war footing. Schacht wanted to slow the pace of rearmament which was sucking in huge amounts of raw materials and upsetting the balance of trade again. Hitler overruled him and launched instead his Four Year Plan with Hermann Goering in charge. It held a new twist to the notion of *autarky*: the introduction of a programme for Germany to produce as many materials as it could for itself, including synthetic oil and rubber. Hitler and Goering, however, played on the theme of *lebensraum* as being the permanent solution to Germany's economic problems. Both of these last points illustrate that *autarky* and *lebensraum* were pseudo-economics which only made sense if seen in the light of their military usefulness. The production of synthetic oil was very expensive – each ton of oil required four tons of coal – costing much more than imported oil which was, however, vulnerable to naval blockade in wartime. *Lebensraum*, as Hitler had defined it, could only be achieved by conquest and would have to be defended – an expensive business in itself.

The evidence and arguments in this chapter show that while the economic problems of the Great Depression did not directly cause the Second World War, they did a lot to create the circumstances in which it could develop. They made nations selfish and inward-looking, too concerned with their own problems to pay enough attention to the developing international political crisis. They created political instability in which ordinary people looked for simple solutions to complex problems. By contributing to the downfall of the Weimar Republic, they gave Hitler his big chance. At the same time, they left other countries unable or unwilling to resist his ambitions until it was too late to avoid war.

TASKS

Notemaking: some tips

The advice given here applies equally to chapter 1 (and other chapters), so go back and make notes on it when you have done this chapter.

1 Chapter 2 is set out in four main sections:

The economic clauses of Versailles
The economic recovery of 1924–9
The Great Depression 1929–33
Hitler's economic ideas and the coming of war

Use these as headings for your own notes.

2 Each section is divided into sub-sections – use these as sub-headings.

3 As you read each sub-section, summarise it in your own words:

A The Reparations Settlement: in 1921 it was decided that Germany must pay for war damage to France (52%), Britain (22%), Italy (10%) and Belgium (8%): a total of 132 billion marks at 2 billion marks a year.

B Disagreement about reparations: the German government claimed this was too much. Some Britons agreed with them but France didn't. Modern historians still can't agree. NB Weimar governments, never popular at home, couldn't afford to be seen to pay up cheerfully.

These will make good notes for revision/essay writing purposes.

4 For last-minute revision, notes can be reduced a stage further to fit each section on to a side of a library index card. For example:

---

1 Economic clauses of Versailles

A <u>Reparations</u>: decided in 1921, Germany to pay France 52%; Britain 22%; Italy 10% and Belgium 8%. Tot. 132 billion marks

B <u>Disagreements</u>: Germans protested – figures too high. Some Brits agreed, French didn't. NB Weimar govts. unpopular already.

C <u>Enforcement</u>: French keenest on payment because of damage to France/ anxious to prevent German revival. Britain worried that reps. hurting German economy, preventing revival of trade with them. German govts. dragged feet until Jan. 1923 French occupied the Ruhr → hyperinflation in Germany: end of attempts to enforce reps. by force.

CHAPTER THREE

DIPLOMACY AND APPEASEMENT BETWEEN THE WORLD WARS

Objectives

◢ To establish the extent to which the Second World War was due to failures in international diplomacy between the wars

◢ To establish the reasons for Appeasement and explain why it failed.

1919 (Oct.)	27 states accept Wilson's idea of a League of Nations
1920 (Nov.)	41 nations at first full session
1920 – 21	Czechoslovakia, Romania and Yugoslavia form 'Little Entente'
1921 (Sept.)	Poland makes pact with Czechoslovakia and Romania
1922 (April)	International economic conference, Genoa
(Oct.)	Mussolini comes to power in Italy
1924 (Nov.)	Ramsay MacDonald's Labour Government in Britain falls
1925 (Oct.)	Locarno Pact signed by Britain, France, Italy and Germany
1926 (Sept.)	Germany admitted to League of Nations
1928 (Aug.)	USA and France promote Kellogg–Briand Pact
1929 (Feb.)	Litvinov Pact
1931 (Sept.)	Manchurian Crisis
1933 (Jan.)	Hitler becomes Chancellor of Germany
(Oct.)	Hitler announces Germany is to leave the League of Nations
1934 (July)	Murder of Austrian Chancellor Dollfuss by Nazis
1935 (Oct.)	Italian invasion of Abyssinia
1938 (March)	German invasion of Austria
(Sept.)	Munich agreement
1939 (March)	German invasion of Czechoslovakia
(Sept.)	German invasion of Poland. Britain and France declare war on Germany

The period between the two World Wars was one of the most complex in diplomatic history. It would take a whole book to detail every pact, treaty and agreement, every twist and turn of each country's attempts to achieve its aims. Each country's diplomacy was interwoven with its economic policies (chapter 2) and its military strategy (chapter 4). So, this chapter is only a 'broad brush' attempt to show the overall picture as faithfully as possible.

Diplomatic aims of individual countries

Their reactions to the settlement divided countries into three groups:

1 Those who wanted to put the war behind them. The **USA** had only reluctantly become involved in European affairs and tried to retreat into its traditional isolationism. **Britain** too always disliked getting too closely involved in the affairs of the rest of Europe. It had made several colonial gains out of the war and now wished to concentrate on its Empire and to restabilise its economy. It had some sympathy for French concern about Germany but disagreed about the best way to deal with this.

2 Those who were less happy with the outcome of the war. **France** had nearly exhausted itself in the effort to defeat Germany. Their fear was that when Germany recovered, it would attack France again and France would no longer be able to resist. France tried to avoid this by insisting on the strict enforcement of German territorial losses, disarmament and reparations. It also sought alliances with other countries who wished to contain Germany: Poland and the 'Little Entente' (see below) and wanted more whole-hearted British support.

Italy and **Japan**, although both had gained territory, were also disappointed by their gains and wanted to revise the terms in their favour. Italy, particularly after Mussolini came to power in 1922, spent the rest of the 1920s pressing Britain and France for 'compensation' in Africa for its disappointment over European territorial gains.

3 Finally, there were the two 'international outcasts': the **Soviet Union** and **Germany**. Both had lost much in the First World War and bitterly resented those losses. Both were feared and mistrusted by the international community: Soviet Russia because of its Communism and Germany because it was blamed for the First World War. Given their contrasting regimes and ideologies and that they had been enemies in the war, they should have been natural enemies but their isolation and mutual desire to revise the peace treaties drove them together in the 1920s.

The League of Nations and collective security

Hopes and fears

The League of Nations was controversial from the start. Ordinary people hoped that it would mean an end to the international anarchy of the past. It looked as though it might be a democratic and effective peacekeeping organisation with a parliament (the Assembly) and a constitution like the democracies who were largely responsible for setting it up. Some politicians also supported it, although not always with the same idealism as the 'man in the street'. French politicians in particular hoped it would support their efforts to maintain the Versailles settlement and stop the spread of Communism.

There was plenty of strong anti-League feeling too. Professional diplomats and soldiers thought that the whole notion was too idealistic and dangerous – its very existence could create a false sense of security and discourage governments from making necessary but expensive defence arrangements. The Senate was worried about American sovereignty – the League might have the power to overrule Congress – and refused to join. Defeated countries like Germany and Russia, who were not allowed to join yet, resented it as a device to prevent revision of the peace settlement.

Inherent weaknesses and difficulties

The founder members comprised 32 Allied powers and 13 neutral states. Its institutions, which met in Geneva in neutral Switzerland, included the Assembly (the League's 'parliament') in which all members had one representative but which only met for a few weeks a year. The Council was a much smaller body, in permanent session, ready to act in a crisis. It began with four permanent members (Britain, France, Italy and Japan) and four elected members. Because all four permanent members were victorious, imperial powers and most of them European as well, the League suffered from a Eurocentric, Great-Power bias. The fact that Italy and Japan were also 'revisionist' powers meant that the League could only act effectively as long as Britain and France cooperated to keep them in check.

The remaining League institutions came in for much less criticism and did a lot of good work: the **Secretariat** was the League's civil service. Its functions were largely routine and non-controversial; the **International Court of Justice** (which met at the Hague in Holland) dealt with legal disputes between members; the **Special Departments** (such as the Mandates Commission and the International Labour Organisation) were created to carry out specific responsibilities on behalf of the League.

The idea of ***collective security*** had several potential weaknesses: the machinery was clumsy and slow; action had to be agreed by the Assembly unanimously (except for the aggressor); economic sanctions would not hurt only the aggressor; and the League had no armed forces of its own.

In the early years after the First World War, the League had to settle several minor disputes. This is its early record:

Date	Dispute between	Nature of dispute	Outcome
1921	Yugoslavia and Albania	Territorial	Occupying Yugoslav troops were forced to leave Albania.
1921	Sweden and Finland	Disputed ownership of the Aaland Islands	The League decided in Finland's favour.
1921	Germany and Poland	Disputed territory in Upper Silesia	The League's plebiscite produced unclear results. Germany felt that the League's interpretation of it favoured Poland.

| 1923 | Germany and France | A strike by German workers in the French-occupied Saar district. | French troops were used to break the strike. |
| 1923 | Italy and Greece | Mussolini was angered by the assassination of Italian officials who were working in Greece. He occupied the Greek island of Corfu to back up his demand for compensation. | The League forced Italy to evacuate Corfu but the Greek government was made to pay compensation. |

KEY TERM

Collective security   Members of the League promised 'to respect and preserve against external aggression the territorial integrity and existing political independence of all members of the League' (Article 10). They also promised to reduce armaments and to settle disputes peacefully. If a member was attacked, all members would apply economic sanctions against the aggressor and, if necessary, resort to joint military action.

How good was the League's record to 1924?

It showed some bias towards two leading League powers (France and Italy) and, perhaps, some anti-German bias. However, it had avoided serious mistakes and produced a solution to every problem. Nevertheless, serious questions remained. How would it cope when a problem arose in which the different British and French views of the League's role clashed? All the disputes described above were European – if there was a dispute elsewhere would the League have the will and the means to deal with it? When a sudden crisis blew up would the League be able to respond rapidly enough?

Early attempts to enforce or overturn the Peace of Paris

Alongside these first actions of the League, those who were dissatisfied with the Peace of Paris began their attempts to change it.

France's alliances in Eastern Europe

Its strongest supporters were France and the new East European states who owed their existence to the Peace of Paris. Hungary felt that it had been harshly treated and, along with Germany and Russia, was a 'revisionist' power from the start. Faced by this trio, the other new states of Eastern Europe – Poland, Czechoslovakia, Romania and Yugoslavia – began to construct a network of alliances with each other and France. Between 1920 and 1921 the three smaller countries (Czechoslovakia, Romania and Yugoslavia) made a series of defensive alliances which became known as the 'Little Entente'. France made a defensive alliance with Poland in 1920 and between 1924 and 1927 a series of agreements of mutual aid in the face of unprovoked attack with each of the Little Entente countries. In 1921 Poland made pacts with Romania and Czechoslovakia. By this network of alliances, France made itself the main guarantor of the Peace of Paris in Eastern Europe.

It is difficult to believe that this 'system' of alliances could really have worked. Their geographical locations created problems for communications and combined military operations. Add to these the mutual suspicion between Poland and the 'Little Entente' countries and the fact that, compared with Germany and Russia, the other East European states were poor with smaller populations, and you may wonder why they bothered. Partly, probably, in an attempt to reassure their own people and, partly, because to do something was better than nothing.

The black sheep flock together

Russia and Germany, the two major outcasts from the international community, drew together in the early 1920s. Early in 1922 a great international economic conference met at Genoa in Italy. All the main European powers took part, hoping to achieve a new agreement on reparations and war debts. America's decision not to attend and France's refusal to negotiate with Russia until it paid its prewar debts to France, however, scuppered all chance of progress. Germany and

Russia, disappointed at the continuing hard-line attitude being taken towards them, made a treaty at Rapallo (near Genoa) on 16 April 1922. It included an agreement on war damage claims between themselves and promises of economic cooperation. There were rumours (later confirmed) that it also contained secret clauses about military cooperation.

Rapallo hardened French attitudes towards Germany over reparations and strengthened the Anglo-French *entente* for a while but also increased British concern that too harsh a policy towards Germany would drive that country into the arms of Bolshevik Russia.

Diplomatic effects of France's attempt to enforce reparations

This issue was important from the diplomatic as well as the economic angle. Having learned from the occupation of the Ruhr that France could not enforce Versailles alone, the French Prime Minister, Edouard Herriot, joined with the British Prime Minister, James Ramsay MacDonald, in promoting the Geneva Protocol in the Assembly of the League. It was an attempt to beef up the Covenant by combining compulsory arbitration, disarmament and further guarantees of the 1919 frontiers. Unfortunately for France, when MacDonald's Labour Government fell from power in autumn 1924, the new Conservative Government abandoned the Protocol.

The Locarno Pact and honeymoon period (1925–9)

Origins of the Pact

The man who had salvaged the German economy, Gustav Stresemann, became the Weimar Republic's next Foreign Minister (1925–9). He realised that constant confrontation with France would hinder Germany's recovery and decided instead to follow a policy of 'fulfilment' of the terms of Versailles in the West, but it would be wrong to see him as having different aims from other German politicians. He knew, for instance, that Germany was breaking the arms limitations provisions and tried to prevent the Inter-Allied Military Control Commission (IMCC) from investigating these breaches. He also clearly intended to turn to the questions of territorial adjustments in the East and the Anschluss union with Austria as soon as the western settlement was sorted out. The difference lay more in his style and attitude. He seemed willing to accept much of Versailles in the West and to talk positively to the British and French governments about reparations and the Rhineland.

In Britain, the new Foreign Secretary, Austen Chamberlain, realised the need to reassure France if the Conservatives were going to abandon the Geneva Protocol. He considered reviving an earlier idea for a treaty which would offer France specific, but limited, guarantees of security. Stresemann heard of this and proposed an international treaty guaranteeing the demilitarisation of the Rhineland (and leading to its evacuation) and the *status quo* in western Europe.

The French responded cautiously – before they could agree to the evacuation of the Rhineland, they wanted Germany to comply with the Versailles disarmament clauses. They also wanted guarantees of the security of their Polish and Czech allies in the East.

It was decided to meet at the lake resort of Locarno in Switzerland in October 1925. The picturesque setting helped to create a cheerful, positive atmosphere for which the *Times* newspaper invented the phrase 'spirit of Locarno'. Even the French and German delegates' discussions were good-humoured. Private, informal meetings between the Foreign Ministers helped to iron out sensitive issues and the Locarno Pact was the result.

The Locarno Pact and its implications

The delegates from Britain, France, Italy, Germany, Belgium, Poland and Czechoslovakia signed eight documents between them. They can be divided into three main parts:

◢ A Treaty of Mutual Guarantee between the first five countries named above, which confirmed Germany's western frontiers – as they had been settled at Versailles.

◢ Various 'arbitration conventions' in which countries promised to settle disputes by peaceful means in future.

◢ Treaties of guarantee between France, Poland and Czechoslovakia in which France promised to protect them against possible future German aggression.

The most significant aspects of the Locarno Pact, however, were the promises that were *not* made. Germany made no promises to accept the *east* European frontiers given it at Versailles. Britain did *not* support the French guarantees to Poland and Czechoslovakia. Even France's own promises to its east European allies carried less weight as now it could only go to their aid if Germany attacked it first.

Britain and Germany had both got what they wanted. Britain had made a guarantee of frontiers rather than committing itself closely to France. It had avoided committing itself to any action in eastern Europe at all. The Pact was not welcomed in Berlin where German nationalists complained that once again a Weimar politician had accepted the humiliating Versailles terms. But in fact the Locarno deals were a great success for Stresemann: Germany had been re-accepted into the international community; it joined the League of Nations in 1926 and was given a permanent seat on the Council. At the start of 1927 the IMCC was wound up and the evacuation of Allied troops began. All this had been achieved without giving any ground on Germany's aims in eastern Europe.

The Locarno honeymoon (1925–9)

The Pact was followed by four years of optimism in European diplomacy and a feeling that Locarno had settled the Versailles terms at least in the West. Austen Chamberlain, Aristide Briand and Gustav Stresemann were awarded the Nobel Peace Prize for their parts in it. The League mediated successfully in disputes between Greece and Bulgaria (October 1925) and Turkey and Britain (acting as the mandatory power for Iraq). Even the Soviet Union began to cooperate with the League's humanitarian and economic organisations.

In 1928–9 two further developments from outside the League, promoted by the USA and the USSR, seemed to bolster the idea of 'collective security'. In August 1928 the USA and France promoted the Kellogg–Briand Pact in which over 60 countries renounced 'aggressive war' as a means of settling disputes. The USSR responded with the Litvinov Pact (February 1929) in which, with four East European neighbours, it also renounced the use of war to settle disputes.

Conclusions

Despite all this apparent progress the title of the next section of this chapter is 'Collective security comes undone' – so what went wrong? There were undoubted weaknesses in the League and the Locarno and later pacts from the beginning:

◢ When Germany joined the League in 1926, it reinforced the tendency for the Great Powers to stitch things up in private and bring a ready-made solution to the Council for approval. The pacts were more symbolic than practical. No provisions were made for any kind of sanctions against those who broke the Kellogg–Briand or Litvinov pacts. Nor was a clear definition of '*aggressive* war' worked out – any teacher will tell you how difficult it is to discover 'who started it' in a playground brawl, let alone an international conflict.

◢ There were signs even during the honeymoon that not everyone believed it would last. France began to build the Maginot Line in 1927. Mussolini was growing increasingly frustrated at his inability to win a genuine revision of the Peace of Paris through negotiations with Britain and France. The 'Little Entente' and Poland remained nervous and pulled closer together.

Nevertheless, perhaps the spirit of Locarno could have triumphed over all these if the Great Depression had not changed the mood of Europe and made countries and people mean-spirited and selfish.

Collective security comes undone, 1929–35

1929 – the turning-point?

The events which led to the failure of the League began in 1929. They included:

◢ the onset of the Great Depression;
◢ the removal of the last treaty restrictions on Germany (apart from disarmament which it was largely ignoring);
◢ the Young Plan which was believed to have settled reparations;
◢ the Hague Conference which agreed to complete the evacuation of the Rhineland by June 1930;

◢ the death of Stresemann in October and thus the end of his policy of fulfilment.

The removal of these restraints meant that extreme nationalist German politicians now felt free to express themselves more openly and violently. It became clear that they detested Poland and would not rest until they had regained all it had taken from Germany in 1919. Weimar Germany began to rebuild its navy. Brüning's government announced its intention to negotiate a customs union with Austria – clearly intended to be the first step towards achieving the long-standing nationalist ambition of union with Austria.

Hitler becomes Chancellor of Germany, January 1933

When Hitler came to power at the head of a nationalist-dominated government (right wing but not Nazi), he used the reflationary economic policies already prepared by Brüning and took care to appear moderate and statesmanlike to foreign politicians. He promised not to try to revise Versailles by force; was careful to avoid getting into a naval arms race with Britain; and signed an agreement with the Pope. Yet his supporters had acted with such violence in the years when they were bidding for power that the governments of Europe were alarmed.

European reactions to Hitler

France had already been alarmed by the increasingly nationalistic tone of German politics from 1929 onwards, especially as the treaty revisions of that year effectively ended its influence over German politics. In 1931 France was only partly reassured when the League supported it in warning Brüning off the customs union with Austria. The **Soviet Union**, under Stalin's leadership, began to look for allies against Germany. It had made a non-aggression pact with Poland even before Hitler came to power. In 1934 it followed this up by joining the League and allying with France and Czechoslovakia. In **Italy**, Mussolini, worried about Hitler's ambitions in Austria, made approaches to France which were reciprocated even more strongly after the murder of the Austrian Chancellor Engelbert Dollfuss by Nazis in July 1934. **Britain** looked with sympathy on the closer relationship between France and Italy.

The Manchurian Crisis

In September 1931 Japan began its invasion of the Chinese province of Manchuria. This was a serious conflict between two members – exactly what the League had been created for. Look back at the earlier section of this chapter on 'Inherent weaknesses and difficulties' of the League of Nations. Can you see why the League found it so difficult to act here? Its Commission of Enquiry blamed Japan and China equally but when the League accepted the report, Japan resigned from it and that was effectively the end of the League's involvement. Manchuria became part of the Japanese Empire.

The League had been slow to react, partly because of its cumbersome machinery for dealing with disputes, partly because of the serious economic problems hitting the major powers. It was reluctant to act out of sympathy with Japan and unable to act because its leading powers had insufficient forces in this remote area. The League had failed its first serious test. Perhaps it would do better if the next crisis was nearer to Europe?

The Stresa Front and Abyssinia

In October 1933 Hitler announced that Germany was also leaving the League because of the failure to make progress at the Disarmament Conference and that Germany would now start to rearm in earnest. The meeting between Britain, France and Italy at Stresa in April 1935 was intended to warn Hitler that they stood firmly against any ideas he might have for rewriting the Locarno Pact or uniting with Austria. They also condemned his announcement of German rearmament.

It was not the solidly anti-German front that it might at first appear. France, looking after its own security, made a mutual assistance pact with Russia in May which upset Britain. Britain, concerned about maintaining its naval superiority, made a naval arms limitation agreement with Germany in June 1935, which broke the Versailles limitations on the German navy and deeply offended Italy and France.

The Italian invasion of Abyssinia on 3 October 1935 finished both the Stresa Front and the League. Britain and France (each with one eye on Hitler and the other on their own colonial empires in Africa) were far more concerned to stay on good terms with Mussolini than to defend an independent African country. The League reacted more quickly than it had done over Manchuria and declared Italy the aggressor only four days after the invasion began. In November, it voted for economic sanctions on Italy.

Yet British and French politicians conspired, in the Hoare–Laval Pact (see chapter 7), to delay the League's actions until the Italian conquest was complete and it was too late to do anything. This plan to give Mussolini most of Abyssinia showed that Britain and France only supported the League when it suited them. Their own publics were outraged and the League was utterly discredited in the eyes of the world. Countries began to revert to old-style defence agreements and alliances.

Britain, France and appeasement

The events preceding the Second World War will be examined in detail in chapter 7. Here we want to examine the reasons and the politicians behind the policy of appeasement.

Britain and appeasement

'Appeasement' was originally a positive concept rather than the expression of contempt that it has since become. Britain's appeasement of Germany and Italy had begun in 1919 and Austen Chamberlain had used the expression to describe the Locarno Pact, as an attempt to remove 'potential sources of friction and conflict through negotiation and the promotion of peaceful change' (British Foreign Office Notes). The difference was that during the 1920s and early 1930s Britain had controlled the process but in the mid 1930s Hitler seized the initiative.

Why appeasement? There is a long list of reasons:

A *The impact of the First World War*: the popular feeling that there must never be another Great War made it difficult for politicians like Winston Churchill who believed that the only way to avoid this was to stand up to Hitler and Mussolini.

B *The economic problems of the interwar years*: the Left in British politics believed that carrying out social reform and reducing unemployment was more important than rearmament. The Wall Street Crash in 1929 increased government reluctance to spend on defence and the Treasury reinforced this by insisting on strict spending limits.

C *Public opinion and party politics*: when, in July 1935, a nationwide opinion poll ('The Peace Ballot') recorded huge majorities in favour of arms reductions and the continued pursuit of collective security, politicians were bound to be influenced. Neville Chamberlain had seen the rapid gains made by the Labour Party and the trade unions in the Great War and was afraid that another war would further advance the power of the Left.

D *The Empire*: the self-governing dominions of the Empire (South Africa, Australia and New Zealand), whose support had been vital in the First World War, were strongly opposed to helping Britain in another war. On the other hand, Britain relied on its imperial trade more than ever.

E *In foreign affairs* there was widespread sympathy for German calls for revision of Versailles, while France's reliability and usefulness as an ally were doubted. Between the wars, France was weak and divided and recovered slowly from the Great Depression. Its will and ability to resist Germany looked doubtful.

F *British military weakness*: in 1935 a secret military report advised the government that the navy would be unable to defend the Empire and support a war in Europe at the same time and that the country was currently incapable of defending itself against air attack. It advised the government to increase defence spending, improve air defence and avoid a simultaneous war against Japan, Germany and Italy.

Figure 6 shows how these factors reinforced each other and all seemed to point in the direction of appeasement.

France and appeasement

France has often been treated unsympathetically by British historians. It has been accused of being paranoid about a third German invasion since 1870 and being divided, weak and unlikely to be able to defend

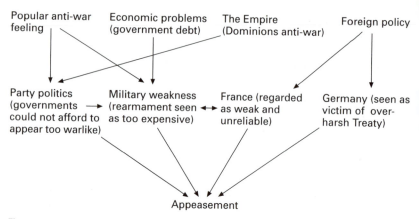

Figure 6 The impact of the First World War on British Foreign Policy in the 1930s

itself. Its surrender after only six weeks of fighting in 1940 seems to prove these accusations true.

Yet there is much evidence to dispute them. Many historians now accept that a second world war was a strong possibility from 1919 onwards. France's fear of Germany, therefore, was not paranoia but a justified fear. It knew also that it could never defeat Germany alone and its foreign and defence policies, preparing for a long drawn-out war, simply reflect this. France's foreign strategy of building a system of allies who would support it while it held the German army at bay behind the Maginot Line (see next chapter) was thwarted by the American retreat into isolationism, the unreliability of Stalin's Russia as an ally and Britain's reluctance until the last moment to make firm promises of support to France. Yes, the French people *were* reluctant, like the British, to face the prospect of another war and with even greater reason. Yet, in the end, in Edouard Daladier they found a politician behind whom most were able to unite and the belated upswing in the French economy in 1938–9 gave them more confidence in their ability to resist Hitler. In the summer of 1939 they were sad but prepared for war – the 'phoney war' of September 1939 to May 1940 sapped their determination.

The role of Neville Chamberlain

We have already looked at the reasons why appeasement seemed an inevitable policy to most British politicians but it is Neville

Chamberlain (British Prime Minister 1937–40) whose name has become synonymous with it.

Chamberlain was a 'conviction' politician. He believed that he had the right policies and could change the course of events by personal intervention. He believed he could do business with Hitler and was not prepared to listen to other points of view, though there were few apart from Winston Churchill who could suggest a clear alternative.

Chamberlain's own political experience led him to believe that appeasement was the *best*, as well as the only, policy for Britain – if it could be made to work. His period as Minister of Health (1924–9) left him haunted by images of Britain's cities, defenceless against air attack. His long stint as Chancellor of the Exchequer (1931–7) left him worried about the ability of the British economy to support another long war.

It is difficult to judge how naive he was. He could have known that Hitler was evil and yet seems to have believed that getting Hitler to sign compromise documents would successfully bind him to keeping his promises. He stepped up Britain's rearmaments programme, partly to lend weight to his own hand in negotiations, partly as an insurance policy in case appeasement failed. And yet he persisted with appeasement when everyone else recognised that it had failed. In the spring of 1939, after the collapse of Czechoslovakia, British public opinion at last decided that Hitler had to be stopped. Chamberlain persisted with trying to appease him in secret. There are objective reasons: the Treasury still felt that the British economy would collapse; the military still lacked confidence in Britain's ability to face more than one enemy at a time. But, probably, having invested so much of his personal credibility in the policy, it was difficult for Chamberlain to recognise that the time had come to stop. His illness (he died in 1940) may also have clouded his judgement. Whatever, he was now caught between two irresistible forces: Hitler's ambitions and a British public which was determined to stand in the way of them. Chamberlain had no choice but to issue an ultimatum to Hitler over Poland.

Roleplay exercise

Now that you have looked at both the economic problems (in chapter 2) and the diplomacy of the interwar years, here is an exercise that brings the two together. It will help you to understand the problems involved in relations between countries when economic and political interests are both highly important but often pulling in different directions.

Divide the set into two groups. One group is the British Foreign Ministry, responsible for Britain's relations with the rest of the world. The other half becomes the Treasury, responsible for the health of the British economy. At a Treasury meeting in 1934, the second group has the task of coming up with a set of proposals on trade designed to promote British economic recovery. The first group, meeting in the Foreign Office, has to work out a policy to deal with the arrival in power of Adolf Hitler in January 1933. Both groups should beware of bringing hindsight into the discussions.

In a plenary session, each group should present its proposed solution. Discussion should centre on the contradictions and divergences in the two sets of proposals.

If you are a large group of students, you could save this exercise until the end of chapter 4 and bring in your defence chiefs to advise you on the feasibility of what the Foreign Office and the Treasury want to do.

CHAPTER FOUR

ARMS AND STRATEGY

Objectives

◢ To establish why – in spite of widespread revulsion after the First World War – it proved impossible to achieve world disarmament

◢ To show how German rearmament led to a general European rearmament.

The 1914–18 War had been so terrible that politicians and other commentators felt they must do whatever they could to prevent future wars or, at least, make them less deadly. President Wilson believed that naval rivalry between Britain and Germany had led to the arms race before the Great War. It had also led to the suffering of millions of innocent victims when the British navy blockaded German ports in a bid to starve Germany into surrender; and the German U-boat (submarine) campaign against merchant shipping in the Atlantic and the North Sea had tried to do the same to Britain. The arms race on land had led to three further factors:

◢ Devoting a huge proportion of government spending to building up and maintaining armed forces was difficult for governments to justify unless they were seen to be necessary.

◢ Military leaders, suspicious that their enemies might become too strong, could urge politicians to start a war while they still had the advantage rather than wait to see whether it would come at all.

◢ The sheer size of the armies and armaments involved had slowed down the pace of the war and increased the number of deaths and amount of destruction.

President Wilson's analysis – placing much of the blame for the war on the arms races – is not accepted by most modern historians. They think that the major cause of the war was aggressive nationalism and that the arms race was just a symptom of this.

During the war, a rapid advance in military technology had led to new weapons whose potential for increasing the horrors of war was enormous. The submarine, which had been used to deadly effect against merchant shipping in the North Atlantic, was the most immediately worrying. It also looked as though it might, eventually, make a surface navy obsolete. This worried Britain in particular. Tanks and aircraft were only used to a limited extent during the war but their capacity for destruction was clear.

The military clauses of the treaties

In Wilson's 'Fourteen Points' he tried to provide solutions to these problems. One idea was disarmament which was to be worked out by the League of Nations.

The Covenant of the League of Nations

This contained a number of Articles (or clauses) designed to prevent armed conflict and to limit the devastation when it did occur. Two of them were particularly important:

◢ Article 8 dealt with disarmament: 'The Members of the League recognise that the maintenance of peace requires the reduction of national armaments to the lowest point consistent with national safety and the enforcement by common action of international obligations'. But how could 'the lowest point consistent with national safety' be defined in specific numbers of troops, tanks and aircraft?

◢ Article 16 laid down what would happen if a state persisted with a conflict against the League's advice. It would be regarded as having gone to war against all other members and, if economic sanctions still failed to halt the conflict, then the Council would notify the Members 'what effective military, naval or air force' they would be required to contribute. These commitments sound impressive but the lack of its own forces and the need to inform and win the assent of Members would affect its ability to respond in a crisis. And would Members always be as keen to carry out the League's requests as was assumed?

Before any of this could be discovered in practice, peace had to be made with the defeated countries. It was made on the assumption that they would be forced to disarm immediately and the victorious powers would disarm voluntarily under the guidance of the League once Europe had settled down.

The disarmament of Germany

Germany was the only Great Power disarmed in the Treaty. The General Staff was to be abolished. The British and Americans, feeling that there was an unhealthy militaristic tradition in Germany, wanted to end German conscription but the French were afraid (rightly as it turned out) that a high-calibre professional army could easily become the officer corps of a new conscript army in the future. The Anglo-American view was adopted, however, and the German *army* limited to 100,000 long-term volunteers. It was allowed no cavalry and no heavy guns, nor was it allowed to develop tanks. All war material was to be handed over to the Allies.

Most of the German *navy* was interned at Scapa Flow in the Orkneys and, while discussions were going on between the victorious powers about its future, it settled its own fate by sinking itself. The size of the German navy in future was limited to 36 ships, mostly small ones (destroyers and torpedo boats) and the largest limited to 10,000 tons. Germany was to have no submarines at all.

The potential of aircraft in warfare had been shown during the First World War and the victors were hastening to develop *air forces*. Once again, Germany was forbidden to do the same, though it was allowed to develop civil aircraft from the mid 1920s onwards. Finally, to ensure that all these disarmament terms were kept, the Inter-Allied Control Commission was set up. These terms created resentment among the German people, to whom an impressive army had been a cause of pride since the seventeenth century. Germany believed that stature and success in European and world politics were closely related to the amount of military 'clout' a country had. Giving up most of their arms made them feel severely diminished, especially as time passed and the other Great Powers failed to disarm.

As part of the general disarmament of Germany, the Rhineland was 'demilitarised' (see Figure 7).

The French wanted to annex the west bank of the Rhine but Wilson and Lloyd George could see that this would make Germany as bitter as

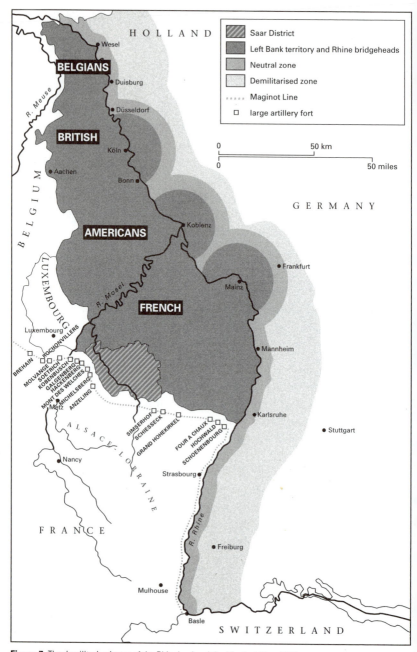

Figure 7 The demilitarised zone of the Rhineland and the Maginot Line, 1919

the French had been over Alsace-Lorraine. Recognising the genuine French fear of a third invasion, they compromised by agreeing on the demilitarisation of the West Bank and a 50-kilometre strip of the East Bank. This meant that the Rhineland would be occupied by Allied troops for the next 15 years and Germany was not allowed to refortify the West Bank even after that. This reassured France to some extent but was a potential source of friction.

Germany's ex-Allies

These were also disarmed. Austria's army was limited to 30,000; Hungary's to 35,000; and Bulgaria's to 20,000. Even at the time, observers were worried that this might not be enough to enable these countries to resist the unrest being stirred up by Russia.

Reactions to the idea of disarmament

◢ Source

To my mind it is idle to impose a permanent limitation of arms upon Germany unless we are prepared similarly to impose a limitation upon ourselves. I recognise that until Germany has settled down ... it is essential that the leading members of the League should maintain considerable forces both by land and sea in order to preserve liberty in the world. But if they are to present a united front ... they must arrive at such an agreement in regard to armaments among themselves as would make it impossible for suspicion to arise between the members of the League in regard to their intentions towards one another. If the League is to do its work for the world it will only be because the members of the League trust it themselves, and because there are no rivalries and jealousies in the matter of armaments between them. Unless this is arrived at ... the League of Nations will be a sham and a mockery ... Unless we secure this universal limitation we shall achieve neither lasting peace, nor the observance of the limitation of German armaments which we now seek to impose.

Lloyd George in his Fontainebleau Memorandum (1919)

If Lloyd George was concerned about the practicability of disarmament, military leaders scoffed at it. They said that the idea that war could be eliminated by international agreement was ludicrous. Indeed, if it created a false sense of security it could be positively dangerous. But because these same military leaders had been so inefficient, unimaginative and callous in their behaviour in the late war, their views went unheeded.

Ordinary citizens seemed to want the League to make disarmament work without entirely believing that it could. Immediately after the war electorates, especially in mainland Europe, were not ready to accept disarmament if this might threaten their ability to defend their frontiers. There was support for the League in France until Georges Clemenceau failed to persuade Britain and the USA to give it its own forces. After that there was heavy pressure on French politicians to enforce the peace terms on Germany which dragged its feet on disarmament until the occupation of the Ruhr showed that this would not work. French opinion then split, with the Left trying to strengthen the League but block disarmament and the Right believing that France should look after its own security. In Britain in 1935 the Peace Pledge Union organised the 'Peace Ballot', to which 11 million people out of 31 million voters responded. They voted massively in favour of 'an all-round reduction in armaments by international agreement' and still by a large majority in favour of military action against any nation found guilty of attacking another. As this was after the Japanese invasion of Manchuria, it is reasonable to assume that these were mostly long-held views. Thus there was clearly a popular desire to do whatever could be done to prevent another disaster like the First World War.

Strategic priorities

Between the wars, then, life was difficult for the armed services in Britain and France. Regardless of public opinion, however, they had to meet the different strategic priorities of their governments. British and French forces both had first to defend the homeland. After that, as an island that was not self-sufficient but a great trading and manufacturing nation, Britain's next priority was to defend its merchant navy; and lastly to defend the Empire. Thus its main concern was a strong navy. France, as a continental state and great agricultural producer, was concerned to protect its empire second and its merchant navy third. Its main concern was its army. This difference was to be very important in the disarmament talks.

Germany's main concern was to delay and avoid disarmament as far as possible. Weimar politicians, especially Stresemann, showed great skill in carrying on secret arms development and in playing on the differences between Britain and France. Once Mussolini had come to power in Italy in 1922, the armed forces became an essential tool of his aggressive foreign policy. He devoted a lot of money and effort to building up all three armed services. Although Russia was too weak to be an immediate threat, it nevertheless had the potential – given its size, non-League status and political beliefs – to completely wreck disarmament once it recovered. This was the background, along with the Great Depression, against which the Disarmament Conferences took place.

The League and the Disarmament Conferences

Naval arms limitation

These talks began promisingly. The Washington Conference of 1922, as well as finalising the peace settlement in the Far East, produced a Naval Armaments Treaty dealing with capital (large) warships. The five signatories – the USA, Britain, France, Italy and Japan – agreed that for the next 10 years none of them would build any warships bigger than 10,000 tons. They also agreed a naval tonnage ratio by which Britain and the USA were allowed 525,000 tons of capital shipping each, Japan 315,000 tons, and France and Italy 175,000 tons.

In 1927 at the Geneva Conference, Britain, USA and Japan failed to reach further agreement on their relative strengths of smaller naval vessels and submarines. In 1930 at the London Conference, however, these three plus France and Italy did agree on limiting the size and use of submarines. Britain, the USA and Japan also agreed to scrap some warships by 1933.

These agreements suggested that disarmament might be possible but there were differences between naval and military disarmament. Battleships were fairly straightforward to define and more difficult to build in secret than tanks, for instance. In 1918 Germany had scuttled its own navy so there were no problems in making it comply with the terms of Versailles. But Germany did drag its feet over reducing its army and weapons to the Versailles limits. At the Spa Conference in Belgium (1920), the Germans admitted that they still had twice the permitted number of soldiers and even greater quantities of artillery and machine guns. From 1922 to 1924 the IMCC (Inter-Allied Military Control Commission) tried in vain to force Germany to disarm. Even by the time of Locarno in 1925, Stresemann had been unable to get the German army to cooperate with the IMCC.

The Preparatory Commission

This was set up against this unpromising background in May 1926. It was made up of all major powers save Russia, which joined it in 1927, and took three years to come up with a proposed convention for discussion at the Conference in 1932. Germany and Russia were unhappy with these proposals because they included the condition that all existing agreements on arms limitations in previous treaties must stand. This meant that the Versailles restrictions on Germany would continue whatever might be decided at the Conference about other countries' arms.

The Disarmament Conference 1932–4

This conference was overtaken by economic, political and military events. Economically, the world was by now in the grip of the Great Depression which made countries more defensive than ever. Politically, the increasingly nationalist German government felt that the time was ripe for a determined push to undo more of the Versailles terms. It was helped by the fact that the three western democracies were divided over what they wanted to achieve: France still wanted to give the League teeth by setting up its own 'police force' for peace-keeping operations, but Britain and the USA opposed this. Militarily, when the 60 nations met in Geneva on 2 February 1932, Japanese troops were already marching through Manchuria.

There was stalemate because of incompatible German and French demands. Germany demanded equality in armaments with the other Great Powers but France would not agree to any reductions of its armaments until its security was guaranteed. There was also interminable argument about what constituted a 'defensive', as opposed to an 'offensive', weapon and how checks were to be kept on whether countries were observing their limits. The Conference adjourned in July 1932.

When it reconvened in February 1933 there was greater optimism. Britain, France and the USA had agreed to make concessions to Germany – but Adolf Hitler was now Chancellor of Germany. First France and then Britain put forward new proposals but neither was acceptable to Hitler and the Conference broke up again in June 1933. In October, when it met again, Britain, France, Italy and the USA announced that they had agreed a four-year arms freeze. After this Germany would be allowed equality of arms but this was too slow for Hitler who demanded immediate equality. He withdrew Germany from both the Conference and the League.

The Conference met again in May–June 1934 but German withdrawal had ended any chance of getting France to agree, especially when Hitler renounced the Versailles limits on German armaments in March 1935.

Rearmament

German rearmament before Hitler

We have already seen how German governments resisted disarmament from the start, but they went further than that. The Reichswehr (German army) was never firmly controlled by the Weimar Republic and its first postwar commander, Hans von Seeckt, proved brilliant at getting around the Versailles restrictions. He set out to turn the Reichswehr into a superb fighting machine by:

- selecting high-quality recruits;
- making secret arrangements for the development of new weapons with German manufacturers and their foreign subsidiaries;
- creating, in 1920, a special department – 'Sondergruppe R' (Special Group Russia) – to organise cooperation with the Soviet Union.

Weimar politicians must have known about much of this (the size of the military budget alone gave it away) but chose to say and do nothing.

By the early 1930s, with the removal of the last foreign control over German policy and the shift to the Right in Weimar politics, Weimar governments themselves began to be more open about rearmament. In 1930 they launched the first pocket battleship, the *Deutschland*. It was just inside the Versailles limits but superbly designed, very fast and with exceptional firepower for its size. It was a signal that Germany intended to become a great naval power again and more such ships followed. Then, in November 1932, during the Disarmament Conference, the War Ministry finalised a plan for a large increase in the army by 1938. So Hitler's rearmament of Germany in the later 1930s was a stepping-up of a process that had begun long before, not something completely new. Indeed, if it had not been for the work of earlier leaders and politicians, it might have taken Hitler much longer to complete his own rearmament.

Hitler and German rearmament

February 1933   Shortly after becoming Chancellor, Hitler outlined his plans to army and navy leaders: to get rid of the hated Versailles military restrictions and then conquer *lebensraum* (chapter 2) in the East for colonisation by Germans. These ambitions required massive rearmament. He moved cautiously at first, waiting for excuses and opportunities to present themselves.

October 1933   The Disarmament Conference, already in session, presented the first excuse. When France and the other Powers refused Germany equal treatment over disarmament, Hitler pulled out of the Conference and the League.

March 1935   Hitler announced the re-introduction of conscription to bring the German army up to 550,000 men and revealed the existence of the Luftwaffe (German air force). By this time, the basis had already been laid for the mass production of military aircraft. The Luftwaffe was especially valuable to Hitler because it gave him the ability to make threats which carried weight. He constantly exaggerated its size for propaganda purposes abroad.

March 1936   Hitler made use of a favourable set of circumstances to risk the **reoccupation of the Rhineland**. Britain and France were preoccupied with the Abyssinian Crisis. The Hoare–Laval Pact (see chapter 7) had made both governments unpopular and they were on poor terms with each other. France's mutual assistance pact with the USSR (May 1935) had upset Britain and Britain's Naval Arms Limitation agreement with Germany (June 1935) had angered France. Hitler ordered the German army to begin preparing for the occupation in December 1935. The German troops that marched into the Rhineland on 7 March 1936 were a token force. Hitler announced that Germany was doing this because of the threat to it from the Franco-Russian Pact. France was between governments and unable to react swiftly even if it had wanted to.

It is often said that this was the point at which Hitler could have been stopped. He was certainly extremely nervous himself and German forces were given orders to retreat if challenged. The people of Britain and France were against taking any action that might lead to conflict, however. British politicians also had some sympathy with Germany's claim that it had a right to defend its frontiers. France was not prepared to challenge Germany without British support. The problem was referred to the League which condemned the German occupation but did no more. Sanctions were still in force against Italy and to extend them to Germany would have hit many economies hard.

August 1936 Goering was given extensive powers to prepare the German army and economy for war within four years.

1936 Both Hitler and Mussolini gave Franco, the Spanish Fascist leader, military support in the Spanish Civil War. It gave the Luftwaffe a trial run in which the value of close air support for ground forces was clearly and frighteningly demonstrated.

March 1938 The German army marched into Austria; and in **March 1939** the German army marched into Czechoslovakia – neither of these involved any fighting and the German army was not bloodied in battle again until the invasion of Poland in September 1939.

What sort of war were the German armed forces ready for when war broke out in 1939? The army of 3.7 million men (700,000 currently in service with 3 million reservists ready for mobilisation) was the best in Europe but had its weaknesses. The best units it had were the armoured (Panzer) divisions that Hitler had started in 1935. On the other hand, the haste in which Germany had rearmed meant that there were shortages of equipment and inadequate training for many of the infantry.

The Luftwaffe (air force) was ready and well-equipped with both bombers and fighters to undertake a number of vital roles:

- destroying enemy air power;
- bombing centres of war production;
- destroying communications (roads, railways, telephone lines);
- supporting the army and navy in battle.

By contrast, the navy was still quite small in 1939, though a plan (Plan Z) had recently been adopted to expand it over the next five years. Thus it was not ready at the outbreak of war either for surface operations in the North Sea or another U-boat campaign against merchant shipping in the Atlantic. Also, the German economy was suffering under the strain of rearmament. All these factors suggest that Hitler did not intend to fight a lengthy world war in 1939 but a short sharp war, or series of wars in Europe.

How the other powers reacted to German rearmament

France

For France, Hitler's arrival in power and rapid rearmament of Germany confirmed their worst fears. They had begun to prepare for it long before he came to power, however, when they began building the Maginot Line, ready for the eventual evacuation of the Rhineland. The Maginot Line was not an unbroken line but a series of defensive strongpoints along the French border with Germany. The French were essentially preparing for a re-run of the Great War: a long drawn-out affair in which they would have to defend France while they waited for Britain and perhaps the USA to come to the rescue again. If you look at Figure 7 on page 68 you will see that the Maginot Line did not continue along the Belgian frontier. This is not a sign of French stupidity in failing to prepare for a repeat of the 1914 invasion through Belgium for, unlike 1914, Belgium was no longer neutral but a defensive alliance with France. For France to build a defensive wall along its Belgian border would be telling the Belgians that it had no intention of helping to defend them. In 1936, however, Belgium ended the alliance with France and the latter began to fortify their common border.

The real problems for France lay in the defensive thinking behind the building of the Maginot Line and in its largely conscript army. France was expecting a German attack in the West as in 1914 – but what if Hitler attacked first in the East? How would France then be able to deliver the aid it had promised the Poles and the Czechs, especially with a half-trained conscript army unsuited to carrying out an aggressive war of rapid movement? France was ill-prepared for the sort of war Hitler seems to have had in mind.

Britain

One British reaction to German rearmament under Hitler was appeasement (see chapter 3). Britain also tried to negotiate with him on naval armaments. The Naval Arms Limitation Agreement allowed Germany to increase its naval strength to 35 per cent of that of the Royal Navy, 45 per cent in the case of submarines. This broke the Versailles and Stresa limits but the British government argued that it was simply a sensible recognition of changing circumstances that protected its naval superiority.

Britain's armed forces reached their weakest point in the interwar period just as Hitler began to rearm. Spending on the armed forces had been held down for economic reasons and because it was unpopular until the failure of the Disarmament Conference in 1934. Even the Royal Navy, traditionally the strongest of the three services, had a fleet of slow, ageing ships. The British army too was less impressive than bald figures make it look. It numbered 390,000 regular (*i.e.* professional, not conscripted) troops but of these only 200,000 were British and the other 190,000 were in the British army in India. There were huge demands on it and it was widely dispersed throughout the Empire. By then the service chiefs were seriously worried: Hitler's rearmament in Europe was a second threat to the Empire. Japan already had Manchuria, was bent on further expansion and obviously had its eyes on the ill-defended British possessions in the Far East.

Rearmament began with the RAF in 1934. This relatively late but timely expansion meant that by 1939 the RAF was fairly well-equipped with new fighters (Hurricanes and Spitfires) with which to defend

Britain, though its bombers were mostly older with a limited range. In 1936 naval rearmament began too but ships take time to build and a lot of the newly-ordered ones were still under construction when war broke out. By the time of the Munich Crisis of September 1938, while Chamberlain was still trying to appease Hitler, British industry was hurriedly producing new weapons in case he failed. Finally, the government introduced conscription in August 1939 though this would make no impact until later in the war. Thus Britain was some way towards being ready to defend itself in the air and at sea but in no position to contribute to the defence of Poland against Hitler in September 1939.

Italy

Mussolini had mixed reactions to German rearmament. He wanted further territorial gains himself, including some from France on both sides of the Mediterranean but he knew that his armed forces were drained after Abyssinia and the Spanish Civil War. The Italian forces' weapons and equipment were now ageing. On the other hand, Mussolini saw how reluctant Britain was to back France in blocking German rearmament and expansion. He resisted the temptation to encourage Hitler and even acted as a restraining influence on him until the outbreak of war. Then he was so impressed by how swiftly Germany overran France that he declared war too, with fatal results for himself and Italy.

The USSR

Theoretically, the USSR had been preparing to support proletarian wars of liberation since its own revolution. Ironically, Stalin's purge of the officer corps from the Red Army in 1937 had compromised even its ability to defend Russia successfully. Stalin rearmed Russia in parallel with Hitler and had a large army and air force ready at the outbreak of war. But Russia was already at war with Japan when the European conflict broke out and, like Britain, wanted to avoid having to fight on two fronts if it possibly could.

The USA

The USA had adopted an even more determinedly non-interventionist stance than Britain. Even after the Japanese invasion of China in 1937 the US government would not coordinate military operations against

Japan with Britain. As in 1914–18, Britain needed to borrow American money and buy equipment from the USA to fight the war but the American government had specifically ruled this out under recently passed neutrality legislation.

Thus no country was fully prepared when war began, not even Hitler's Germany.

Essay on causation

Why did it prove impossible to achieve general disarmament between 1919 and 1934?

This is a 'causation' question. Most questions that begin with the word 'Why' are causation questions and there is a straightforward formula that you can apply to them.

You need to look for a **list** of causes – as complete a list as you can think of.

Then you must try to work out their **relationship** to each other and, if possible, work out some kind of rank order of importance. Begin by looking for a list of reasons for the failure of disarmament (in causation questions, if you find yourself stuck, it sometimes helps if you try to think of Circumstances, People – individuals, groups like parties or even whole countries – or Events that had some bearing on the question).

When you have made your list, give it a **structure** – this is a more coherent or logical way of using it than just a list. There are various ways of doing that with this particular question. You could organise it under the three sections given above – that is, Circumstances (begin by looking at the underlying problems), People and Events (with the last event being Hitler's rise to power which finally put an end to all hopes of disarmament) – or, as this essay spans 15 years, you could treat it chronologically. If you take this approach, however, beware of falling into the trap of just 'telling the story' of those years instead of really answering the question. Or you could take the question one country at a time (*i.e.* why was France so awkward about disarmament; why did Britain show so little enthusiasm, etc?) – or you could look at the causation diagram for the policy of appeasement in chapter 3 (Figure 6) and try to construct a similar one for this question. Is any of these better than the others – if so, why?

There is no perfect format for an A-Level essay but it does need (a) to be as complete as you can make it, and (b) to show that you have thought about it and really are trying to answer the question, not simply writing down everything you know about it.

CHAPTER FIVE

HITLER AND THE CAUSES OF THE SECOND WORLD WAR

Objectives

◢ To examine the continuing historical debate about Hitler's aims in foreign policy

◢ To decide if Hitler had consistent plans or just seized opportunities as they presented themselves

◢ To decide if Hitler was aiming at European or world domination

◢ To judge Hitler's policies by what he said or wrote about them

◢ To conclude whether Hitler intended to start the Second World War.

Did Hitler really intend to start the Second World War?

What Hitler hoped to achieve in foreign policy has divided observers and historians ever since he came to power. There are several strands to the debate:

◢ Did he have any consistent aims or plans or did he just seize whatever opportunities came his way?

◢ Was he aiming at European or world domination for Germany?

◢ Did he jump or was he pushed (*i.e.* were his foreign policies the result of his own aims or were they forced on him by external factors)?

◢ Should we judge his policies by what he said and wrote about them, by what he actually did, or both?

Mein Kampf

The question above is just one aspect of this debate, although all the points mentioned above relate to it. Before you can understand the controversy you need some idea of what Hitler wrote about his ambitions in foreign affairs and the problems associated with these sources. The first major account Hitler gave of his intentions was *Mein Kampf* written in prison in 1924. The book consisted of 700 pages and was not mainly about his foreign policy, though it does contain specific goals. The *Anschluss* (union) with Austria was laid out on the first page, perhaps unsurprisingly when one remembers that Hitler was Austrian himself in origin.

◢ Source A

Only a sufficiently large space on this earth can ensure the independent existence of a nation ...

Germany today is not a world power ... The National Socialist movement must seek to eliminate the present disastrous imbalance between our population and the area of our national territory, regarding the latter as the source of our food and the basis of our political power. And it should strive to eliminate the contrast between our past history and the hopelessness of our present political impotence ...

The demand for the restoration of the frontiers of 1914 is a political absurdity of such proportions and implications as to make it appear a crime. Apart from anything else, the Reich's frontiers in 1914 were anything but logical. In reality, they were neither final in the sense of embracing all ethnic Germans, nor sensible with regard to geo-military considerations ... We are putting an end to the perpetual German march towards the south and west of Europe and turning our eyes towards the land in the east. We are finally putting a stop to the colonial and trade policy of the prewar period and passing over to the territorial policy of the future.

However, when we speak of new land in Europe today we must principally bear in mind Russia and the border states subject to her. Destiny itself seems to wish to point the way for us here ... The colossal empire in the east is ripe for dissolution ...

Today we are not struggling to achieve a position as a world power; we must fight for the existence of our fatherland, for the unity of our nation and the daily bread of our children. If we look around for European allies from this point of view, only two states remain: England and Italy ...

On the coldest and soberest reflection it is at the present time primarily these two states, England and Italy, whose most natural selfish interests are not, at any rate essentially, opposed to the German people's requirements for existence and are indeed to some extent identified with them.

*Adolf Hitler, **Mein Kampf** (1922)*

Hitler goes on to set out in detail his plans to invade the Ukraine and to exterminate its population to make room for German colonists.

(You should attempt the questions in Set 1 (page 95) before moving on.)

Hitler's second (or secret) book

The second example of Hitler's writings, which is often quoted by those trying to assess his aims in foreign policy, is his second (or secret) book of 1928. It concentrates more on foreign policy than *Mein Kampf* but largely repeats the same themes: anti-semitism; *lebensraum*, which would entail war against Russia and possibly France; hope of alliances with Britain and Italy.

Hitler returned to the theme of *lebensraum* in many speeches from 1928 to 1933 when he came to power. After that he stopped talking about it in public, possibly because he was trying to impress other countries with his moderation and statesmanship, at least until he had consolidated his position. He returned to the theme on several important private occasions, the first being on 3 February 1933 in his first address to naval and military chiefs when he talked of: 'the conquest of new living space in the East and its ruthless Germanisation'.

Probably the best known (and most controversial) exposition of the *lebensraum* policy is in the *Hossbach Protocol* of November 1937. Colonel Hossbach was Hitler's adjutant at a secret conference with his army advisers in November 1937. After the meeting, Hossbach decided that what Hitler had said was so important that he would make a copy of it from his minutes of the meeting and from what he could remember. Thus it is not an official document but a second-hand, or even third-hand, account. Nevertheless, it is a detailed version of how Hitler thought things might go over the next eight years.

◢ Source B

Hitler hoped to explain to the gentlemen present his basic ideas concerning the opportunities for the development of our position in the field of foreign affairs ...

The aim of German policy was to make secure and to preserve the racial community and to enlarge it. It was therefore a question of space. The German racial community comprised over 85 million people and, because of their number and the narrow limits of habitable space in Europe, constituted a tightly-packed racial core such as was not to be met in any other country.

(Hitler then went on to discuss and dismiss, as possible solutions to the need for space, *autarky* and participation in the world economy.)

The only remedy ... lay in the acquisition of greater living space – a quest which has at all times been the origin of the formation of states and the migration of peoples. That this quest met with no interest at Geneva or among the satiated states was understandable ... The history of all ages ... had proved that expansion could only be carried out by breaking down resistance and taking risks; setbacks were inevitable. There had never in former times been spaces without a master and there were none today; the attackers always came up against a possessor.

The question for Germany ran: where could it achieve the greatest gain at the lowest cost?

German policy had to reckon with two hate-inspired antagonists, Britain and France, to whom a German colossus in the centre of Europe was a thorn in the flesh, and both countries were opposed to any further strengthening of Germany's position either in Europe or overseas ...

Germany's problem could only be solved by means of force and this was never without attendant risk ... If one accepts as the basis of the following exposition the resort to force with its attendant risks, then there remain still to be answered the questions 'When?' and 'How?'. In this matter there were three possible outcomes to be dealt with:

Case 1: period 1943–5. After this date only a change for the worse, from our point of view, could be expected ... Our relative strength would decrease in relation to the rearmament which would by then have been carried out by the rest of the world ... If the Führer was still living, it was his unalterable resolve to solve Germany's problem of space at the latest by 1943–5.

Case 2: if internal strife in France should develop into such a domestic crisis as to absorb the French army completely and render it incapable for war against Germany, then the time for action against the Czechs would have come.

Case 3: if France should be so embroiled in war with another state that it could not 'proceed' against Germany ... Actually, the Führer believed that most certainly Britain, and probably France as well, had already tacitly written off the Czechs and were reconciled to the fact that this question would be cleared up in due course by Germany ... An attack by France without British support was hardly probable.

... the annexation of Czechoslovakia and Austria would mean an acquisition of foodstuffs for 5 to 6 million people ... The incorporation of these two states with Germany meant ... a substantial advantage because it would mean shorter and better frontiers, the freeing of forces for other purposes, and the possibility of creating new units up to a level of about 12 divisions, that is, one new division per million inhabitants.

*Abridged version from Adolf Hitler, **The Hossbach Protocol** (1937)*

Try the questions in Set 2 on page 95 before proceeding.

Hitler's secret speech, February 1939
This final example of Hitler's own words about his aims and methods in foreign policy comes from a secret speech to a gathering of senior officers on 10 February 1939.

◢ Source C

All our actions during 1938 represent only the logical extension of the decisions which began to be realised in 1933. It is not the case that during this year of 1938 – let us say – a particular action occurred which was not previously envisaged. On the contrary all the individual decisions which have been realised since 1933 are not the result of momentary considerations but represent the implementation of a previously existing plan, though perhaps not exactly according to the schedule which was envisaged ... It was also quite obvious that the Austrian and Czech problems would have to be solved in order further to strengthen Germany's political and, in particular, its strategic position. To start with I was not quite sure whether both problems ought to be or could be solved simultaneously or whether one should deal first with the question of Czechoslovakia or with the Austrian questions. There was no doubt that these questions would have to be solved and so all these decisions were not ideas which were realised at the time of their conception, but were long-made plans which I was determined to realise the moment I thought circumstances at the time would be favourable.

The task questions for Source C are on page 95. The last question is a very important one. If we believe that Hitler was telling the truth on most of the occasions when he talked about foreign policy, then it is certain that he had some kind of plan which would involve a large-scale war sooner or later, and there is no argument. If, however, when you looked at Set 2 question 5 you decided that Hitler had no interest in whether his actions were right or wrong, then what guarantee is there that he would tell the truth on any occasion? This leads us to ask: What reasons would he have for lying? Look at the next source in the light of that question.

Who or what to believe

◢ Source D

Ciano stood up to Hitler very energetically. He had received detailed instructions from the Duce (Mussolini) to point out to Hitler the 'madness' of embarking on war. He more than once pointed out that a war with Poland would not be confined to that country. This time, the Western democracies would certainly declare war. During the meeting the next day, Hitler said: 'I am convinced that neither England nor France will embark upon a general war.'

> Notes made by Paul Schmidt, Hitler's interpreter, at a meeting between Hitler and Ciano, the Italian Foreign Minister and Mussolini's son in law, on 11 August 1939 about three weeks before the outbreak of war

This document can be interpreted in different ways, depending upon the reader's point of view. If Hitler had a detailed plan to obtain more *lebensraum* in the East, then this was the obvious next step after gaining Austria and Czechoslovakia. He was also sticking to his belief that Britain and France would not intervene to save Poland. It could also be the next step to world domination. On the other hand, if Hitler was an opportunist with no moral scruples, he could be simply trying to convince Galeazzo Ciano that Italy should enter the war because he needed Italian support, regardless of whether he believed that Britain and France would resist. Other historians would ask what pressures were pushing Hitler into this policy. Apart from the economic problems noted earlier in this chapter and in chapter 2, you may remember the German hatred of Poland (described in chapter 3), caused by the loss of land and the division of Germany by the Vistula corridor given to Poland to allow it access to the sea. Hitler had promised to right this injustice and was under political pressure to do so.

Thus, even simply reading Hitler's own accounts raises some important questions. We know he was consistent in stating his desire to achieve *lebensraum* to the East of Germany, and at the expense of Russia. But we also know he would be prepared to lie when it suited him. Also, we have seen that some of Hitler's statements can be used to support either the theory that he had a clear idea of what he wanted to achieve or the opposite, that he was chiefly an opportunist. And isn't there a danger that if we focus too much on what Hitler wrote that we may get a one-sided picture of his importance in deciding foreign affairs?

How then can we decide who or what to believe? It is not a question of searching for 'the truth' but of looking to see which arguments we find the most convincing. To do this we need to trace the argument from the beginning, to see why different interpretations were put forward and, where it is possible, to find agreement.

Until shortly before war broke out in 1939, contemporary politicians and others did not know what to make of Hitler. Chamberlain, although he didn't like Hitler, treated him for a long time as a politician not all that different from himself. He tried to buy him off with appeasement and to tie his hands by getting him to sign the Munich Agreement over the future of Czechoslovakia. During Hitler's early years in power even Winston Churchill was not as certain what to make of him as he later claimed.

◢ Source E

It is not possible to form a just judgement of a public figure such as Adolf Hitler until his life-work as a whole is before us. History is full of examples of men who have risen to power by employing grim and even frightful methods but who have been regarded as great figures whose lives have enriched the story of mankind. So may it be with Hitler.

*Winston Churchill, **Great Contemporaries** (1935)*

When he wrote his own account of the Second World War in 1948, Churchill seemed to be using the benefit of hindsight when he wrote of the 'obvious' nature of Hitler's plans:

◢ Source F

When eventually he (Hitler) came to power there was no book (Churchill is writing about Mein Kampf) which deserved more careful study from the rulers ... of the Allied Powers. All was there – the programme of German resurrection; the technique of party propaganda; the plan for combating Marxism; the concept of a National-Socialist state; the rightful position of Germany at the summit of the world.

What had changed Churchill's and others' interpretations of Hitler was their experience of the events just prior to and during the Second World War. The Germans, under Hitler's leadership, had plunged the world into a second world war and committed atrocities that it was impossible to believe had been ordered by a sane human being or carried out by a civilised nation. Historians who lived through the war were influenced by the necessary but all-pervading anti-Nazi propaganda of the period and the popular revulsion that followed the revelations of the Holocaust (Hitler's attempt to exterminate European Jews) and other Nazi atrocities. As Alan Bullock wrote in the preface to the revised edition of his book *Hitler: A Study in Tyranny* (1962): 'No man can sit down to write about the history of his own times – or perhaps of any time – without bringing to the task the preconceptions which spring out of his own character and experience. This is the inescapable condition of the historian's work, and the present study is no more exempt from these limitations than any other account of the recent past.' This led to the theory of Hitler as an evil genius who had hypnotised and led astray a basically decent but politically naive people.

Writers like Alan Bullock and Hugh Trevor-Roper went to Hitler's prewar and wartime writings and speeches and found abundant evidence that he had a long-term programme with fixed goals and a fairly well worked out path towards them. They decided that these goals and ideas such as anti-semitism, German racial superiority, *lebensraum* and world domination were Hitler's own and not a part of traditional German politics. The following extract is a good example of this interpretation.

◢ Source G

Hitler's war aims are written large and clear in the documents of his reign. They are quite different from the aims of the men who, in 1933, admitted him to power and who, after 1933, served him in power. They are also, in my opinion, different from the aims which have been ascribed to him by historians who regard him as a mere power-loving opportunist ...

Mein Kampf ... is the expression of a political philosophy fully formed ... The importance of Mein Kampf as a real declaration of Hitler's considered and practical war aims, even in 1924, is often overlooked ...

Thus from 1920 to 1939 Hitler's aims were clear: repudiation of colonies, repudiation of old imperial frontiers (those, he said, were an ambition 'unworthy of our revolution'), and instead the creation of a revolutionary, nationalist force able to conquer permanently 'the great continental space' of Russia. In the face of this reiterated clarity, it seems odd to me that distinguished historians should insist that Hitler had no consistent war aims ...

Of course it is true that, at different times, Hitler was prepared to say almost anything, and we can never believe anything to be true merely because he said it. However, since some of his statements of aims must have been true, even if at other times contradicted by him, we cannot reject everything out of hand: we must find a criterion of veracity (truth). Now I believe that such a criterion is easily found. Hitler's statements of his aims can be accepted as true provided they are explicable ... first, as part of a general philosophy regularly expressed even in adverse tactical circumstances, and secondly, by long term practical preparations. Once we apply these tests ... only the philosophy of an eastern empire remains ...

Thus to the end Hitler maintained the purity of his war aims. To him, from 1920 to 1945, the purpose of Nazism was always the same: it was to create an empire, to wrest the 'great continental space' of Russia from the Russians ...

Thus Hitler's ultimate strategic aims can be detached with absolute clarity, with absolute consistency, from the tactical necessities or concessions which surround them ... In 1923 France, in 1940 England stood between him and his goal. But these were not his real enemies ... In 1939 he would make 'the greatest gamble of his life': the Russo-German Pact. But all these were tactical necessities.

Hugh Trevor-Roper, **Hitler's War Aims** (Macmillan, 1960)

(You should attempt the questions in Set 4 (page 96) before proceeding.)

New interpretation

The consensus, that Hitler had a definite programme with clear goals including things that would ultimately lead to another great war, was shattered in 1961 by the publication of A. J. P. Taylor's *The Origins of the Second World War*. Taylor argued that Hitler was really a supreme opportunist with only the vaguest idea of what he wanted to achieve and had no detailed plans for achieving *lebensraum* at the expense of the USSR (as Trevor-Roper said) or world domination (as Churchill said).

This is what Taylor wrote about Hitler's intentions regarding war:

◢ Source H

Far from wanting war, a general war was the last thing he (Hitler) wanted. He wanted the fruits of total victory without total war; and thanks to the stupidity of others he nearly got them ...

This is not guesswork. It is demonstrated by the record of German rearmament before the Second World War or even during it. It would have been obvious long ago if men had not been blinded by two mistakes. Before the war they listened to what Hitler said instead of looking at what he did ... Until the spring of 1936 German rearmament was largely a myth ... For one thing, Hitler was anxious not to weaken his popularity by reducing the standard of civilian life in Germany (which much-increased rearmament would entail). More important, Hitler would not increase taxes and yet was terrified of inflation ... Most important of all, Hitler did not make large war preparations simply because his 'concept of war did not require them'. 'Rather he planned to solve Germany's living-space problem in piecemeal fashion – by a series of small wars' (Klein). This is the conclusion at which I also arrived independently from study of the political record, though I suspect that Hitler hoped to get by without war at all ... The one thing he did not plan was the great war attributed to him ...

From the spring of 1936, Hitler put some reality into it (rearmament). His motive was principally fear of the Red Army; and of course Great Britain and France had begun to rearm also. Hitler in fact raced along with the others, and not much faster. In October 1936 he told Goering to prepare the German army and German economy for war within four years, though he did not lay down any detailed requirements. In 1938–9, the last peacetime year, Germany spent on armaments about 15 per cent of its gross national product. The British proportion was almost exactly the same.

A. J. P. Taylor, **The Origins of the Second World War** (Hamish Hamilton, 1961)

Taylor's reinterpretation stimulated a new debate. His approach suggested that Hitler's foreign policy was, at least in part, a response to a factor external to Hitler: instead of a fixed programme, what Hitler did was partly determined by the European diplomatic situation. When this produced an opportunity to advance German prestige, power or wealth, Hitler simply grabbed it.

(Now try the questions in Set 5 on pge 96.)

Structuralism and Functionalism

Other historians, also from the 1960s onwards, sought to further widen the debate by arguing that Hitler's foreign policy was determined by other external factors than just the European diplomatic scene. This new school of thought has become known as the 'Structuralist' or 'Functionalist' interpretation. Structuralism means that the structure or nature of the regime that Hitler had created shaped the direction of his conduct of foreign affairs. Functionalism means that his foreign policy was a function, or largely a result, of other factors. Either way, these historians have forced us to consider the role and influence of other offices, institutions and individuals in Nazi foreign policy. There are too many of them to mention – West German as well as British historians – but their ideas of who or what influenced Hitler may be summed up as:

- the expectations he had raised among the German people in his bid for power, such as full employment and improved standards of living, and a more successful foreign policy;
- strong forces in German political, social and economic life (such as German big business, the aristocracy or the officer corps of the German army);
- the economic crises that hit Germany in 1936 and 1938–9;
- pressures from groups and individuals, such as Goering and Ribbentrop, within the Nazi movement;
- pressures from abroad, such as the Great Depression and the rearmament of the Red Army by Stalin.

Here is one example of this school of thought:

◢ Source I

The Third Reich was the first modern state to face the many new problems raised by permanent full employment and was totally unfitted to solve them: the Nazi party had been brought to power to end unemployment, and in the later 1930s the government proved unable to make the great reappraisal and reorganisation necessary to cope with its success ... the built-in need of the totalitarian regime to obtain consent and loyalty and continuous adulation of those classes of society which had most reason to hate it, disabled it from effective intervention in the labour market until internal crisis made such intervention essential and external crisis had provided the necessary justification.

Tim Mason, **Some Origins of the Second World War** (Macmillan, 1964)

The Intentionalist response

Those who have continued to believe that Hitler was the prime mover in Nazi foreign policy, now known as the 'Intentionalist' school of thought, have responded to the work of the Structuralists/Functionalists in two ways. They have tried to refute their arguments and to develop more flexible theories of their own.

Refuting the Functionalists' arguments

The argument that successive economic crises forced Hitler into an increasingly aggressive foreign policy is rejected on the grounds that both crises were caused substantially by Hitler re-orientating the German economy to prepare for war. The crises were the *result* of his preparation for war, not the *cause* of it.

The Intentionalists have produced evidence that suggests that Hitler only took the advice of Goering, Ribbentrop and others when it fitted his intentions and ignored them when it didn't. When powerful groups in German society opposed him, Hitler tightened his hold over them, as he did with the German army officer corps in 1938. Key decisions, taken by Hitler himself, often had to be pushed through against the opposition of powerful groups – the decision to worsen relations with the USSR from 1933 on, the 1934 Non-Aggression Pact with Poland, the Sudeten Crisis of 1938 and the invasion of Poland in 1939. All of these met considerable opposition from one powerful group or another.

As for being the prisoner of expectations that he had raised – domestic pressures did contribute to the character and timing of some of Hitler's foreign-policy initiatives but this was mainly in the early years of the regime when he was less firmly in control. Hitler does seem to have believed that war could be made to pay, could prop up the German economy and its people's standard of living.

The Stüfenplanners

West German intentionalist historians, beginning with Hillgrüber in 1963, have advanced the notion that Hitler had a *Stüfenplan* (stage-by-stage plan) to achieve world domination:

- ◢ Stage 1   Control of Europe;
- ◢ Stage 2   Control of the Middle East and British colonies;
- ◢ Stage 3   World domination which would involve war with the USA.

They find evidence to support this theory in his plans for naval expansion (Plan Z, mentioned in chapter 4) and grand architectural plans. However, most historians think that they go too far, especially with the second and third stages, for which the evidence becomes increasingly thin.

A consensus?

So where does all this leave us? Is it possible to find common ground on which most, if not all, historians agree? At the moment, the intentionalist interpretation, with some modifications, is that favoured by most historians. Under pressure from the functionalists, intentionalists have conceded that Hitler, while he had firm aims, was prepared to be tactically flexible. The driving forces of his foreign policy seem to have been his racial beliefs (Aryan supremacy, hatred of the Jews, contempt for the Slavonic peoples of Eastern Europe); the need for *lebensraum* for the German people; and his varying attitudes to Britain and the USSR.

Hitler took the key decisions in foreign policy himself but did he intend to start a world war in 1939? Here is a final brief extract from a contemporary historian. Richard Overy is considering the question of the purpose of the Nazi economic recovery of 1932–8:

◢ Source J

… the answer was German imperialism and war. Historians disagree about what kind of war it was supposed to be, or the extent to which the economy was actually prepared for war, but there is no disagreement that the German economy was being prepared for some degree of military expansion. From 1932 to 1936 … rearmament was only a small part of the strategy. From 1936–9, that during the period of full employment,

the priority switched to war preparation. The change in economic strategy was signalled by the second Four Year Plan set up in October 1936, which gave Goering responsibility for reorientating the economy for war and achieving self-sufficiency in essential war materials – oil, rubber and steel ... In 1937–8 military expenditure increased to 10 billion marks, in 1938–9 to 17 billion or 17 per cent of GNP. In addition much of the public investment that was not directly military was used for synthetic or substitute production whose purpose was to increase Germany's ability to wage war. When compared with any other major industrial power the proportion of the German economy geared to war was very significant.

Richard Overy, **The Nazi Economic Recovery 1932–8** *(CUP, 2nd edn, 1996)*

Overy hints, in his account, and Taylor argued strongly, that Hitler didn't intend to start a large-scale war in 1939. If you take another look at the state of preparedness of the German armed forces in 1939 (chapter 4 page 75), this evidence tends to back them up. It looks as though Hitler expected or hoped to be able to pick off his opponents one at a time in a series of short, sharp wars. It had been done before in modern German history by Bismarck between 1864 and 1870. But does this reduce his responsibility for the war, if it was the result of a miscalculation?

(Try the questions in Set 6 (page 96) now.)

There was only space here for a quick gallop through a most complex historical debate, which continues today. If this has whetted your appetite, there are excellent books on the subject listed in the 'Further reading' at the end of this book.

TASKS

Try to answer the following sets of questions which relate to the sources provided in this chapter.

Set 1 (Source A)

1 What references are there here to the ideas of *autarky* and *lebensraum* that we considered in chapter 2?
2 Why is Hitler so contemptuous about German demands for undoing the terms of the Treaty of Versailles?
3 What veiled reference is there to the *Anschluss*?
4 Which Great Power(s) was he likely to have to fight to carry out these policies?
5 Which Great Powers does he hope may become Allies, or at least not oppose Germany?
6 List Hitler's aims, as set out in this extract, by summing up your answers to questions 1–3.

Set 2 (Source B)

1 a What foreign policy aims does Hitler outline in this document?
  b How consistent are they with what he had written in *Mein Kampf*, the Second Book and his private speeches 1928–33?
2 Which countries does Hitler see as likely to oppose his aims and how likely were they to go to war against him, in his estimation?
3 What evidence is there in this document to support the theory that Hitler was bent on world domination (look especially at the final paragraph)?
4 What evidence is there to support the argument that Hitler was an opportunist?
5 What evidence is there of any morality (a sense of right and wrong) in Hitler's thinking?

Set 3 (Source C)

1 What is there, in this document, to support the theory that Hitler had a blueprint (a detailed plan) for his foreign policy from the start?
2 What is there to support the theory that Hitler was an opportunist?
3 Is Hitler telling the truth in this document or is he just trying to make it appear that he had been more in control of events than he really had?

Set 4 (Sources D–G)

1 According to Trevor-Roper (Source G) did Hitler have the same aims as other German politicians?

2 According to Source G, what were Hitler's aims? How far does Trevor-Roper's assessment of them agree with Churchill's (Source F)?

3 How does Trevor-Roper deal with the problem of finding out when Hitler was telling the truth? (Source G paragraph 4 – see also sources D and E)

4 How does he overcome the objection that Hitler sometimes did things that seem to contradict the theory of a fixed long-term goal, such as the 1934 Pact with Poland, the 1939 Non-Aggression Pact with Russia and war against Britain in 1940?

5 To what extent is this interpretation based on:

a what Hitler wrote and said,

b what Hitler did,

c Trevor-Roper's own beliefs (paragraphs 1 and 4)?

6 If we accept this interpretation, how likely were Hitler's aims to lead to a world war eventually?

Set 5 (Source H)

1 What evidence does Taylor produce to support his theory that Hitler did not intend to start another world war?

2 To what extent, according to Taylor, was Hitler's foreign policy influenced by considerations other than his personal ambitions?

3 To what extent is Taylor's interpretation based on:

a what Hitler wrote and said,

b what Hitler did,

c Taylor's own beliefs (paragraph 2)?

4 Compare your answers to the last question to your answers to question 5 in Set 4. Can you see where the differences in interpretation come from?

Set 6 (Sources I and J)

1 How many of the factors listed above Source I are mentioned or hinted at in Source 1?

2 Compare Overy's analysis in 1996 (Source J) with A. J. P. Taylor's in 1961 (Source H). Where do the two sources agree and differ?

CHAPTER SIX

THE ROAD TO WAR IN THE FAR EAST AND THE PACIFIC

Objectives

◢ To look at the countries involved in the origins of the conflict in the Far East and the Pacific

◢ To establish when and why the USA and Japan entered the Second World War

◢ To analyse the events in the Far East and the Pacific leading up to the outbreak of war

◢ To decide how far the outbreak of war in the Far East and the Pacific was due to Japanese ambitions and aggression.

Origins of the conflict before 1914

Before the First World War three European countries had long-established colonial empires in the Far East: Great Britain, France and Holland. Three new colonial powers challenged them for influence and trade there in the second half of the nineteenth century: Germany, Japan and the USA. Russia, too, was expanding eastwards towards China and the Pacific. Economic rivalry between these seven powers was increased by the state of the Chinese Empire, which was less and less able to control its territories yet still a great source of wealth. Although they stopped short of outright conquest and annexation, the powers set about acquiring long leases on important Chinese ports and monopoly trading rights with neighbouring provinces. These rivalries played a large part in the outbreak of the Pacific War that turned the European conflict, begun in 1939, into a second world war in 1941.

Japan

In the 1850s this island nation had been threatened with being exploited by the Western Powers in the same way as China. Recognising the danger just in time, Japan had turned itself around remarkably, adopting a more modern political system and beginning a programme of economic reforms. By the turn of the century, Japan had regained control of its own economy and become an expansionist power itself. Japan grew increasingly frustrated, however, at its inability to hang on to territorial conquests in the face of opposition from western rivals. After the Sino (Chinese)–Japanese War of 1894–5, in which they had driven the Chinese from Korea, the intervention of Russia, France and Germany forced Japan to return many of its gains to China, though it kept Formosa (now called Taiwan). A decade later, in the Russo–Japanese War (1904–5), Japan dealt Russia a series of crushing naval and military defeats. When it called in the USA to mediate the peace at the end of the war, however, Japan again had to be content with modest gains – increased influence in Korea, the Liaotung Peninsula and the southern half of the island of Sakhalin to the north of Japan.

By this time Japan was beginning to be taken seriously by the rest of the world. In 1902, Britain made an anti-Russian Alliance with Japan. There was still some way to go, however, before Japan could rank as a world power. By the start of the twentieth century, Japan had really only just begun its industrial revolution. Economic progress and political reforms sat uneasily alongside a largely unchanged society where the armed forces were not firmly under political control and the Emperor was believed to have divine power.

The United States of America

For the USA, involvement in the Pacific and Asia had come about in an apparently less aggressive way. Since the Napoleonic Wars, America had been able to concentrate on its internal affairs. It had become the world's leading economy and had had the potential to become a world power since the end of the Civil War in 1865. America only became interested in questions of power when its trade in the Pacific was threatened by the growth of German and British interests there. Gradually, the USA acquired bases in the Pacific – Hawaii (from 1875) and Pearl Harbor (1887) – and in the Spanish-American War of 1898 its first colonies in the Pacific were won by right of conquest: the Philippines and the island of Guam. The USA also built up its navy to the third largest in the world. The public mood in the USA remained isolationist but its huge financial and economic interests in both Europe and the Far East made it increasingly difficult for it to stay aloof from world affairs.

THE ROAD TO WAR

Perhaps the difference between the attitudes of these two countries can be seen most clearly from the way they reacted to the outbreak of the First World War: Japan saw it as an opportunity for further expansion; while the Americans struggled unsuccessfully to avoid getting involved.

America and Japan in the First World War

Japan entered the war on 23 August 1914 at Britain's request. It seemed an opportunity for Japan to take over Germany's interests in the province of Shantung and some German islands in the Pacific with the blessing of the Great Powers for once. In May 1915, after successful campaigns, Japan pressured the Chinese government into recognising its claims to southern Manchuria and Shantung. Japan's obvious desire to gain further control over the Chinese government, however, alarmed America which began to regard it as something of an Asian bully and tried to limit its gains in the Paris settlement.

In the summer of 1918 there was another episode with significance for the future. Again acting with Allied approval, Japanese forces played the leading role in the Siberian Expedition. Officially, its purpose was to rescue Czech forces which were strung out along the Trans-Siberian Railway; but Japan was really more interested in preventing the creation of a Communist regime in Russia close to its own interests in Manchuria and Korea. The Czechs soon extricated themselves but Japanese forces stayed in Siberia until 1922. This episode led the Japanese to lose some of their awe of Europeans: they saw Russian forces behaving with extraordinary savagery and Russian refugees in a desperate plight. It also gave some of their younger officers a taste for political intrigue which resurfaced in the 1930s.

America, by contrast, stayed out of the war until 1917 but by then had sold and loaned so much to the Allies (US trade with them had increased by 400 per cent between 1914 and 1916) that it could not afford to see them lose. The German declaration in January 1917, of unrestricted submarine warfare on all shipping trading with the Allies, gave President Wilson the excuse he needed. He broke off diplomatic relations with Germany and then declared war on it on 2 April. German encouragement of Mexico and Japan to fight the Americans strengthened anti-German feeling in the USA. Once America threw its weight behind the Allies, victory was just a matter of time.

In suing for peace on the basis of the 'Fourteen Points' (see chapter 1), Germany hoped to divide the Allies. Lloyd George and Clemenceau were too wily to allow this to happen but the ploy did succeed in making it more difficult for the Allies to agree on a satisfactory peace.

The USA and the Pacific from 1918 to the 1930s

Wilson's performance at the Paris peace talks and America's reaction to it were considered in chapters 1 to 4. If you check back over 'The American standpoint' and the 'League of Nations' (chapter 1); 'The Dawes Plan', 'American loans to Germany' and the Young Plan (chapter 2); 'The League of Nations' and the Kellogg-Briand Pact (chapter 3); and Naval Arms Limitation and the League Disarmament conference (chapter 4), you will see that America's withdrawal into isolation was limited by its need to support the European countries in which it had invested so heavily.

There certainly was a powerful isolationist mood in America, most of whose people felt throughout the interwar period that it had been a mistake to enter the war. The US government, however, was less hostile to the outside world. After Wilson's attempt to establish a 'New World Order' by creating the League of Nations had been vetoed by Congress, later presidents had to move more cautiously. They still played an important role in international affairs. American 'observers' attended meetings of the League Assembly in Geneva and America joined the International Labour Organisation under Roosevelt in 1934. Both US politicians and many of its people also showed enthusiasm for disarmament.

The Washington Conference of 1921–2 was the first major international conference held in the USA. It had two purposes: to limit naval armaments (see chapter 4); and to ease the growing tension in the Far East. Thus two treaties were signed at Washington:

◢ The Four Power Treaty (Britain, France, Japan and the USA): the signatories agreed to accept each other's possessions in the Pacific and to consult each other in the event of aggression there. This treaty replaced the Anglo-Japanese Treaty of 1902, to American satisfaction and Japanese resentment.

◢ The Nine Power Treaty: all countries (barring the Soviet Union which was not invited to the conference) with an interest in China agreed to respect its integrity (*i.e.* not try to take over parts of the country for themselves) and to maintain an 'open door' policy for trade.

The treaties did not succeed in defusing the tension because:
- no machinery was created to ensure that either was upheld;
- they tried to ignore the Russian presence in the Far East;
- the Japanese resented American treatment of them from 1919 onwards.

Nevertheless, isolationism among the public continued until the end of the 1930s when Congress passed a series of Neutrality Acts (1935–9), designed to make it impossible for President Roosevelt to involve America in any future conflict in the way that Wilson had in 1917. American reaction to Japanese aggression towards China from 1931 onwards was, therefore, muted and Roosevelt had to act carefully in gradually aligning himself with Britain and France against the Axis Powers and Japan.

Japan 1918–30

Foreign affairs

In the years immediately after the First World War, Japan increasingly resented American treatment. Japan had been disappointed with its gains in the Peace of Paris and had to give up most of its gains in Shantung as part of the Washington agreements. It had failed, because of opposition from the USA and Australia, to get a racial equality clause included in the League's Covenant. The Washington ratio which allowed Britain and the USA to build five capital ships each to Japan's three, left it with an inferior naval status. The Asian exclusion clause of the 1924 American immigration law also made Japan bitter.

Relations with the USSR and China were also causing worries by the end of the decade. The USSR was recovering under Stalin's leadership. Chinese Nationalist forces under Chiang Kai Shek were threatening to regain control of Manchuria.

Political problems

After a postwar period of increasing liberalism in Japan, internal problems were also beginning to surface. There were powerful competing forces in Japanese politics: the political parties (backed by rival big business groups), the Genro (a council of elder statesmen), the senior ranks of the civil service and the armed forces (which were not securely under political control). The political parties were uninspiring: there was bribery and corruption, and proceedings in the Japanese parliament sometimes resembled a noisy brawl. The armed forces were unhappy about the continuing drive for disarmament and resented both the Washington Conference restrictions on naval building and the 1930 London Naval Conference which extended those restrictions from capital ships down to cruisers. Among junior officers, concern about the threat from Russia and Chinese nationalism led to the growth of extreme nationalist ideas there too.

Economic problems

Japan was unable to feed its population from its own land alone and regarded Korea and Manchuria on the mainland as its lifeline. In 1927 it suffered a short-lived economic crisis caused by the bankruptcy of about three dozen banks. This event rocked the confidence of the public in Japanese politicians and their associated big businesses. When the Great Depression itself hit Japan, it led to an alarming fall in overseas trade, especially the silk trade on which many peasant farmers relied to raise their income to subsistence level and whose main purchaser had previously been the USA.

The results of economic crisis, together with a loss of confidence in politicians and the threats to Japanese interests on the mainland, led to the gradual breakdown of political control in Japan. The initiative passed into the hands of the military leaders with their extreme ideas.

The Manchurian Crisis

The attack on Mukden, the Manchurian capital, by the Japanese army of Southern Manchuria in September 1931 followed years of growing friction there. In 1928 the Chinese warlord of Manchuria had been assassinated near Mukden. It was strongly suspected (but not confirmed until after the Pacific War) that this had been carried out by Japanese officers based there. The assassination was intended to signal the start of an invasion of Manchuria but it received insufficient support from senior officers. Over the next three years, however, Japanese control of the South Manchurian Railway came under increasing threat from the Chinese Nationalist forces and a second plot was hatched by local Japanese officers. This time it received more support from General Staff Headquarters in Tokyo.

They staged a 'bomb attack' on the South Manchurian Railway near Mukden, which they claimed was the work of Chinese soldiers. This gave them the pretext they needed to attack the Chinese forces in Mukden itself and Changchun, further north, on 19 September 1931. In spite of the suspicions of the rest of the world, all this was done without the knowledge or approval of the Japanese government. There had, in fact, been a complete breakdown between the civil and military powers in Japan where events had strengthened public support for the military. The core of the army came from the peasant classes who had suffered most from the fall in silk prices. In 1932 a failure of the rice crop in northern Japan created famine among the peasants there.

As Japanese forces fanned out across Manchuria, China appealed for help both to the League of Nations and the USA, as a signatory of the Nine Power Treaty and the Kellogg-Briand Pact. The USA condemned Japanese aggression and announced that it would not recognise any gains made as a result, but that was all. The League also responded cautiously. It sent a Commission of Enquiry under a British chairman Lord Lytton to investigate the situation but – as the British government were not willing to act either (they and the USA were the only powers with large naval forces in the area) – it was really unable to do much. When the Lytton Report – diplomatically but clearly – put the blame on Japan, the latter withdrew from the League early in 1933.

Meanwhile, in Manchuria, Japan had set up the puppet state of Manchukuo, under Pu Yi the last emperor of China, and tried without success to convince the world that it was a genuinely independent new kingdom. In Japan itself, the conquest of Manchuria had loosed a wave of nationalist feeling. It was hoped that control of the province would help to solve Japan's population problem and feed its starving people: compare this with Hitler's ideas on *lebensraum* and *autarky* from Chapters 5 and 2. World disapproval only served to strengthen this instinctive patriotism and Japan fell increasingly under the control of its military leaders.

The Sino–Japanese War 1937

Events in Japan and China 1933–7

Inside Japan, the years between the invasion of Manchuria and the full-scale Sino–Japanese War were dominated by a power struggle between two factions in the army: one that argued in favour of a Japanese advance into Russian territory; the other with the same belief about China. It seemed to have been agreed that Japan would follow aggressive expansionist policies on the Asian mainland, the only disagreement was about the identity of the victim.

The year after the creation of Manchukuo, Japanese troops advanced into Inner Mongolia, in northern China. Japanese political and commercial penetration of northern China followed rapidly. To some extent they had to, for by now Japan was more diplomatically and economically isolated than Nazi Germany had been prior to the outbreak of the war in Europe. Japan had trapped itself in a situation where its own isolation drove it forward into conquering territory in order to survive economically. It was able to do so unchecked for so long because for most of the world's powers these were the worst years of the Great Depression when they were more concerned with solving their own economic problems than supporting China against Japanese encroachment.

This situation began to change in 1936–7. The anti-Chinese faction in the army won the struggle in 1936 in a mutiny which brought down the government. Now preparations to equip Japan for a full-scale war against China were rushed forward. The armed forces claimed nearly

0 per cent of all state spending and the only limit was what the apanese economy could support. It attempted to deal with its diplo-matic isolation by making the Anti-Comintern Pact with Germany in)ecember 1936. This protected its north-west flank against a Russian ittack if its own forces advanced south into China. By 1935–6, how-:ver, the other Great Powers with interests in the area had recovered :nough to resume support of China.

American reaction to Japan's expansion into China

This came in two parts: governmental and popular. When Roosevelt)ecame President in March 1933, peace was already beginning to break Jown. Japan's occupation of Manchuria had changed the balance of)ower in the Pacific. It had broken the 1922 Washington agreements ind the promises it had made more recently in the London agreements n 1930. Japan formally renounced both in 1934. The American gov-:rnment began a gradual diplomatic realignment. In November 1933 it granted diplomatic recognition to the USSR, partly in the hope that it might become an ally against Japan. Roosevelt had to act cautiously, not to say deviously, on occasions because public opinion in the USA reacted to the gathering storm clouds by growing more pacific and iso-lationist. Nevertheless, there was no attempt to appease Japan as there was Germany in Europe. Other Powers joined America in refusing to recognise Manchuria.

The outbreak of war

The Sino–Japanese War began in July 1937 when fighting broke out between Japanese and Chinese troops near Peking (now Beijing). By the autumn, although there had been no official declaration of war by Japan, there was fighting in the north of China and around Shanghai. In December, after advancing up the Yangtze River, the Japanese entered the Nationalist Chinese capital of Nanking. Attacks by the Japanese on British and American ships in the battle zone brought them to the brink of war with those two powers. Profuse Japanese apologies defused the situation but after 1937 most powers were more sympathetic to China, especially after news of Japanese atrocities against the Chinese population reached the outside world. Japan had expected Chiang Kai-Shek, the Chinese Nationalist leader, to surrender after the fall of his capital and was surprised when he decided to fight on.

The road to the Second World War in the Pacific, 1937–41

It took four years for the war between Japan and China to widen into a conflict between Japan and the other world powers. This was partly because of the approach and outbreak of war in Europe – neither Britain nor France had the military capacity to fight a war in Asia as well – and partly because the neutrality laws in the USA still tied Roosevelt's hands. Thus the Brussels Conference of 1937, in condemning Japanese aggression against China but going no further, only encouraged the Japanese army to believe that the colonial powers were too weak to stop them.

Japan reacted to its isolation in two ways:

1 After it had captured Hankow and Canton, the Japanese Prime Minister declared 'A New Order' in Asia in November 1938 and tried to build up Japanese authority throughout the continent. Japan promoted the doctrine of Pan-Asianism in Japan and the parts of China it controlled. It claimed to be fighting for Asia to regain control of its own affairs, free from western political and economic influence. Asian culture with its supposed emphasis on social harmony, community and spirituality was contrasted with western materialism, individualism and inhumanity. The propaganda failed to convince the Chinese who wanted the West to counter Japanese power.

2 It moved closer to the Axis powers. Hitler recognised Manchukuo as independent in 1938, thus giving his approval to Japanese expansionism. This policy too was only a partial success. Japan was shocked by the announcement of the Nazi–Soviet Non-Aggression Pact in August 1939, which nullified the German support against the USSR it thought it had achieved by signing the Anti-Comintern Pact (see page 118 for definition) with Hitler in 1936.

By the time war broke out in Europe in September 1939, there was already fighting going on between Japan and Russia along the Manchurian–Mongolian border and American economic sanctions were in place against Japan. Nevertheless, Germany's string of rapid victories in the spring of 1940 enticed Japan into abandoning its original neutrality towards the European conflict. It signed the Tripartite Axis Pact in September, thereby binding itself to Germany and Italy.

While all this was going on in Europe and Asia, the situation in America had been gradually changing. Roosevelt had begun to discuss future naval cooperation with Britain in December 1937 and gained Congress's approval to expand the American navy in May 1938 and air defences in 1939. In line with public opinion, America remained neutral when war broke out in 1939 but was alarmed by the fall of France in May 1940. German submarines operating out of ports on the French Atlantic coast could now threaten US shipping in the Atlantic as they had done in World War One.

Gradually, Japanese aggression brought about an alliance against it, known as the ABCD Coalition (America, Britain, China and the Dutch). In the spring of 1940 Japan stepped up its attack on China. It pressed Britain into closing the Burma Road (the chief supply route to the Nationalist Chinese forces) and the French Vichy government (collaborating with the Nazis) into granting Japan bases in the north of Indo-China. In America, Roosevelt's position was strengthened by victory in the 1940 Presidential election in which his campaign had been dominated by foreign affairs. He stepped up American support for Britain in Europe: this aid to the enemies of Japan's Axis Allies increased the probability of a future war between Japan and the USA. American sanctions against Japan were gradually increased as its forces moved further south and US aid to China also mounted. Roosevelt also pushed Britain into reopening the Burma Road. For a long time, however, Japan remained wary of attacking the USA out of fear that if it did, this would tempt Russia into attacking it along the Manchurian border.

The events that removed this fear and eventually brought all-out war between Japan and the ABCD Coalition were the Japanese–Soviet Neutrality Pact of April 1941 and the German invasion of Russia that followed two months later. Now that Russia had its hands full with the German invasion from Europe, Japan no longer felt threatened by it. From this point things moved rapidly to war.

In July 1941, Japanese forces occupied bases in southern Indo-China which had belonged to France. From there they were a direct threat to Siam (now Thailand), Malaya and the Dutch East Indies. This provoked an almost immediate – and, as far as Japan was concerned, unexpected – reaction from America, Britain and the Netherlands. They imposed an immediate embargo on trade with Japan, froze Japanese assets held abroad and the USA closed the Panama Canal to its shipping.

Japan now had to choose between giving up its expansionist ambitions or going to war against this coalition of colonial powers. Only the Japanese army leaders felt confident they could win and the government attempted to negotiate peace with the USA. The talks broke down when the latter insisted on Japanese withdrawal from China which would mean giving up everything Japan had gained since 1937. So on 26 November, the Japanese Cabinet supported the army's call for war. On 7 December Japan launched attacks against Pearl Harbor, Hawaii, Siam, Malaya, the Philippines and the Dutch East Indies. The devastating attack on the US navy in port at Pearl Harbor united American opinion against Japan and the USA declared war on Japan on 8 December. Japan's Axis Allies – Italy and Germany – declared war on the USA on 11 December. The world was now at war in the Pacific as well as Europe and its colonial empires.

TASKS

In chapter 1 the Peace of Vienna of 1815 was used as a yardstick against which to measure the Peace of Paris in 1919. Here is a similar exercise, comparing the causes of the Second World War in the Pacific (1941–5) with those of the war in Europe (1939–45). Construct a table like the one below. (All the information on Japan is in this chapter, but the chapters with information on Germany are indicated in the table.)

Japan	Factor	Germany
	Reaction to the outcome of the First World War	Chapter 1
	Impact of the Great Depression on their economies (industry, agriculture, trade)	Chapter 2
	Diplomacy (relations with other countries between the wars, especially those towards which they felt resentment)	Chapter 3
	Their armed forces (relations with the government; attitudes and ideals of leading officers; reactions to disarmament)	Chapter 4
	Their political leaders: ambitions, abilities, beliefs	Chapter 5
	Political systems/régimes: level of political maturity of people and parties	Chapters 1 to 3
	Immediate causes of war	Chapter 7

1 What are the most striking similarities revealed by this table?
2 What important differences are also revealed?
3 Are the similarities enough to prove that war was inevitable in these circumstances, or could war have been avoided in either case?
4 How much blame should the 'status quo' powers (*i.e.* the old-established colonial powers like Britain, France and the Netherlands) take for the Pacific War? Was it all down to Japanese aggression in the end – or what about the other expansionist powers in the area, the USA and the USSR?

CHAPTER SEVEN

EVENTS THAT LED TO THE OUTBREAK OF WAR

Objectives

◢ To focus on the short-term causes of the Second World War of the mid to late 1930s

◢ To decide the point at which the Second World War became inevitable.

The Second World War had long-term and short-term causes. The long-term causes include these factors from chapters 1 to 5:

◢ German, Italian and Japanese dissatisfaction with the Peace of Paris left them determined to 'revise' it in their favour. They were frustrated by their failure to achieve this by negotiation.

◢ The unsolved economic problems after the First World War were worsened by the Great Depression which made states concentrate on their own interests instead of considering their international impact.

◢ The failure of normal diplomatic processes to cope with extremist leaders like Hitler and Mussolini.

◢ The failure of the Disarmament Conference to bring about a general limitation of armaments.

◢ Hitler's ambitions of reversing the Treaty of Versailles and acquiring *lebensraum* in Eastern Europe.

All of these helped to provide the preconditions for another massive conflict but they were not enough on their own to provoke it.

This chapter focuses on the short-term causes of the mid to late 1930s and considers at what point War became inevitable.

Short-term causes

The Japanese invasion of Manchuria in 1931

This has been seen, with the benefit of hindsight, as the first of the chain of crises which led directly to the outbreak of the Second World

War. It was not so obvious at the time but it did clearly heighten inter-national tension when states were already worried about how to cope with the Great Depression at home. The League of Nations' failure to stop Japan worried small countries around the globe and shook people's faith in collective security. It also worsened the already slim chances that the Disarmament Conference, meeting in Geneva 1932 to 1934, might succeed. In particular, it concerned the other countries – like Britain, France and the USA – who had colonial and trading interests in and around China. With the League accepting the Lytton Commission's report and Japan's resignation from it in February 1933, this crisis had not really ended before the next ominous development occurred.

The rise of Nazism in Germany

The changing face of German politics had been causing concern abroad ever since 1929. The death of Gustav Stresemann, the Weimar Republic's most able politician, coincided closely with the removal of the last Versailles restrictions (apart from disarmament) on Germany and the onset of the Great Depression. This led to the growth of parties on the extreme left (Communist) and right (Nazi and Nationalist) who claimed to have simple but drastic solutions for Germany's problems. The loss of public support for these movements, together with their own violent behaviour, made it impossible for the pro-Weimar parties to form stable governments. Thus began a vicious spiral, with each loss of credibility or control by a Weimar government leading to further support for the extremists.

Once he had become Chancellor in January 1933, Hitler posed as a moderate statesman. Perhaps the 'Night of the Long Knives' purge of 30 June 1934 should have alerted people at home and abroad to the true nature of the new regime in Germany. Hitler moved against his rivals inside the Nazi Party and settled old scores outside it, ordering the murders of several hundred people. Nevertheless, the purge of some of the more extreme elements of the Party won Hitler the sup-port of the Reichswehr (German army) and the true facts were carefully concealed from the German people.

Outside Germany, many political leaders could not believe that Hitler intended to follow the crude and outrageous policies he had put forward in *Mein Kampf* a decade earlier. Even Winston Churchill was willing to give Hitler the benefit of the doubt at first. Thus, in general, although countries were already worried by the extreme nationalism of German politics and the evidence of secret rearmament, they did not see Hitler's accession to power as dramatically worsening the situation. His behaviour towards the Disarmament Conference did not greatly change their perception. Those who say that it was obvious what Hitler intended to do from the start and that action should have been taken against him before he had a chance to rearm are arguing with the benefit of hindsight.

The failure of the Disarmament Conference

The Disarmament Conference opened at Geneva on 2 February 1932. Earlier agreements on naval armaments – at Washington in 1922 and London in 1930 – had encouraged a belief that military disarmament might also be possible (see chapter 4). Apart from the facts that circumstances were less favourable and that military disarmament was far more complex than naval disarmament, what ruined the Conference's chances appeared to be not Hitler's extremism, but French intransigence. Understandably, French politicians would not consider disarmament until they were given guarantees of French security. Even when, after pressure from Britain and America, France offered equality of armaments for Germany within four years, Hitler did not appear too extreme in insisting on immediate equality. When he further withdrew his delegates from the conference and Germany from the League altogether in October 1933, the fault still seemed to many to lie partly with France.

The German Non-Aggression Pact with Poland

This was signed in January 1934. It was the first move in German foreign affairs originated by Hitler. It confirmed French worries that Hitler meant them no good in the long run because the ten-year Pact wrecked France's system of alliances in eastern Europe where Poland had been its chief ally. To other powers, however, this agreement seemed to be a sign that Nazi Germany could be settling down into following a normal diplomatic policy: surely Hitler wouldn't have made such a pact with Poland if he really meant to carry the policy of *lebensraum* in eastern Europe or to take revenge on Poland for German losses to it at Versailles?

The failure of the Nazi *putsch* in Austria, 1934

In July 1934, following strong private encouragement from Hitler, the Austrian Nazi movement attempted to seize power in Vienna. The Austrian Chancellor Engelbert Dollfuss was murdered but the *putsch* quickly collapsed. Combined pressure from a suspicious Mussolini and France forced Hitler to disown the *putsch* and act more cautiously towards Austria for a while.

In early 1935, after this reverse in 1934, Hitler was able to achieve a couple of easy propaganda victories:

- January: 90 per cent of the population of the Saar district voted in a plebiscite to return from French to German rule.
- March: Goering announced the existence of the German air force and the reintroduction of conscription.

The latter led to the formation of the Stresa Front by Britain, France and Italy and much diplomatic condemnation but no physical opposition. There was some sympathy in Britain and Italy for the 'unfairness' of continuing German disarmament after the failure of the Conference.

The Italian invasion of Abyssinia

The event that really began the transformation of European diplomacy in Germany's favour, however, was the Italian invasion of Abyssinia. This was a turning-point in the interwar period in several ways:

1 It marked the end of Mussolini's attempts to revise the Peace of Paris by diplomacy. By negotiating with Britain and France, he had been 'compensated' for Italy's meagre war gains with some impressive-looking but largely worthless pieces of African territory. He was frustrated at his failure to achieve more. His policy of gaining influence in Abyssinia since the early 1920s had also failed because of the political wiliness of the Abyssinian Emperor Haile Selassie. There were growing economic problems at home too, from which Mussolini needed to distract his people's attention. All these factors contributed to the decision to provoke war with Abyssinia. The secret order for the 'total conquest' of Abyssinia was issued in December 1934.

2 It also changed how Mussolini was seen by the rest of Europe (see

Figure 8). From a braggart who, nevertheless, usually worked through normal diplomatic channels, Mussolini became seen as the man who had let all hell loose upon the world. The use of advanced weapons and poison gas bombs against the poorly-armed Abyssinian forces; a campaign of terror against the civilian population; the orders to shoot all rebel prisoners – all these showed him to be much more ruthless than many foreign observers had thought until then.

3 It destroyed the credibility of the League of Nations, already badly damaged by its failure to act decisively over Manchuria. Britain and France, desperate to keep Mussolini as an ally against Hitler, tried hard to find a 'compromise'. While they promised to support the League in applying sanctions to Abyssinia, the British and French Governments sponsored a 'Pact' (December 1935) which entailed giving Mussolini control of most of Abyssinia. This satisfied neither the members of the League nor the peoples of Britain and France who forced their governments to abandon it. It also failed to appease Mussolini who would settle for nothing less than total

THE MAN WHO TOOK THE LID OFF.

Figure 8 David Low's cartoon 'The man who took the lid off', *Evening Standard*, 1934

control of Abyssinia. Once he had achieved this, in May 1936, Britain and France urged the League to abandon sanctions on the grounds that there was no longer any point to them.

4 It led to a reorientation of Mussolini's position in Europe. He despised Britain and France for their weakness in trying to please him but he was diplomatically isolated. Germany, however, had behaved as a friendly neutral and he began to look on Hitler more favourably. The Abyssinian crisis is the point at which the two central European dictators began to align themselves against the western democracies and the USSR.

German reoccupation of the Rhineland

In March 1936, during the last stages of the Abyssinian Crisis, Hitler militarily reoccupied the Rhineland. The German army was not ready to confront military opposition and the German High Command and Foreign Ministry both opposed the move but Hitler promised that the German forces would retreat at the first sign of French resistance. He was gambling that the Abyssinian Crisis and France's internal divisions would prevent it and Britain from mounting effective opposition.

The failure of the Hoare–Laval Pact the previous December had left both parties with little enthusiasm for future joint action. France decided not to oppose any future attempt to reoccupy the Rhineland but to support the League of Nations. The League was, however, demoralised and unable to act and diplomatic protest was the worst that Hitler encountered.

This was another turning-point in interwar international relations. It meant the end of the Versailles and Locarno agreements about Germany's western frontiers; and France had surrendered, without a fight, the strategic advantage that a buffer zone with Germany gave it. On the other hand, Hitler's successful gamble raised his prestige in Germany enormously and made it more difficult for the army leaders to oppose him in future.

The Spanish Civil War

This began as an army revolt in July 1936, led by disgruntled generals (notably General Francisco Franco), against the left-wing Republican government which had won the February 1936 elections. It quickly developed into a full-scale civil war when some sections of the army stayed loyal to the government. Overseas interest in this internal power struggle was aroused by what appeared to be a clear left–right split that mirrored the divisions in interwar Europe:

	Republicans versus	Nationalists
led by	Azaña	Franco
and		
supported by	Communists Socialists	Monarchists Catholic Church

Azaña appealed to the French Government for help but it was reluctant and in no position to help unless supported by Britain. Both France and Britain were suspicious of the Communist-backed Spanish Republic and still desperately hoped to keep Mussolini away from Hitler. Anglo-French intervention on the Republican side seemed likely to provoke Italo-German intervention on the Nationalist side. So they organised the 'Non-Intervention Committee' in London, at which 27 states agreed not to supply either side.

It failed. Although Germany and Italy joined the Non-Intervention Committee, they both aided Franco, at first in secret but increasingly blatantly. Hitler hoped to gain Spanish supplies of the minerals he needed for German rearmament if Franco won and he used the aerial support he gave the Nationalist side ('the Condor Legion') to try out the Luftwaffe's new planes and pilots. Italy, who gave far more aid to Franco, by contrast gained less. It was mainly another prestige exercise on Mussolini's part and drained the Italian economy.

Although the war lasted three years, it was clear by early 1937 that, with continued support from the other Fascist countries, Franco would eventually win. The Republic was supported only by Stalin in Russia, though France seriously considered entering the war in 1937. Public opinion in Europe was shaken by the evidence of the appalling destruction inflicted by German Stuka dive-bombers on Republican towns and cities.

The war affected all the European Great Powers from 1936 on:

◢ France and Britain both stepped up their rearmament programmes in 1937. France, in particular, after Belgium had pulled out of the defence agreement they had made in 1920, began to increase its fortifications along their joint frontier. At the same time, the evidence of how devastating aerial bombing could be also made Neville Chamberlain redouble his efforts to appease Hitler and Mussolini.

◢ Stalin, in the USSR, concluded that the liberal democracies were timid and, perhaps permanently, enfeebled. This may have been influential in his decision to conclude the Nazi–Soviet Pact in August 1939, rather than support the democracies against Hitler initially.

◢ Hitler was encouraged by the feeble Anglo-French reactions to both his reoccupation of the Rhineland and the Spanish Civil War.

◢ Mussolini's continued support for Franco left Italy feeling isolated and thus increasingly reliant on Germany.

The formation of the Axis and Anti-Comintern Pact

By 1936, then, Europe was largely aligned in two Great Power alliances, as it had been before the First World War, though the USSR did not belong to either camp yet. The growing closeness of Nazi Germany and Fascist Italy was formalised by Mussolini's declaration of the Axis in November 1936. The Italo-German agreement was officially called the 'October Protocols' but Mussolini called it 'an Axis around which can revolve all those European states with a will to collaboration and peace'. Included in its terms was an understanding that in return for German support for Italy, the latter would no longer oppose German control over Austria.

Three weeks later, against the advice of German diplomats, Hitler signed the Anti-Comintern Pact with Japan.

This was supposedly directed against the activities of the ***Comintern*** rather than the USSR itself but it enabled Germany and Japan to show the rest of the world that they were not as isolated as had been thought. In November 1937, after Mussolini had visited Germany earlier that autumn and been deeply impressed by the military and other displays that Hitler had laid on, Italy also joined the Pact and in December withdrew from the League. Now there were three extreme nationalist, militarist, revisionist Great Powers who had all withdrawn from the League, in alliance with each other. The Pact seemed to pose a threat to the British and French colonial Empires in the Far East as well as the Soviet Union.

KEY TERM

Comintern was the organisation set up by the new Communist government in Russia soon after the Revolution. In keeping with Karl Marx's predictions and Lenin's expectations, its role was to help to provoke the 'proletarian revolutions' that would break out around the world. It was active in China at this time.

The Sino–Japanese War

The outbreak of the Sino–Japanese War in 1937 showed that the signing of the Anti-Comintern Pact had more than a symbolic significance as far as Japan was concerned. The Great Depression had convinced Japan, as it had Hitler, that it was dangerous for a country to become too reliant on international trade. Its leaders set out to build up a sphere of economic influence in China, taking advantage of the Great Powers' preoccupation with their own economic problems. By 1935–6, when the Powers felt able to support China again, Japan decided to launch an all-out attack on it. A clash between Japanese and Chinese soldiers near Peking in July 1937 rapidly escalated into full-scale war.

The outbreak of hostilities here clearly suggested a Japanese threat to the European and American colonial and economic interests in east Asia. It exposed the fragility of the positions of Britain and France – neither had the power to fight a European and an Asian war simultaneously. Thus both tried to avoid confrontation with Japan in view of the precarious situation in Europe.

The *Anschluss*

With Mussolini no longer prepared to protect Austria, the Austrian Chancellor, Kurt von Schuschnigg, came under increasing pressure from Hitler to include more Nazis in his government. When he failed to go far enough to satisfy Hitler, the latter mobilised the German army. When there was no support from Italy, Britain or France,

Schuschnigg resigned. German troops marched into Austria to an enthusiastic welcome. Hitler proclaimed the achievement of the long-held dream of German nationalists: the *Anschluss*, the union of the two chief German-speaking countries, Germany and Austria.

This was his greatest achievement to date: capturing the imagination of the German people and greatly increasing his personal prestige, as well as adding to German manpower. It was of tremendous strategic importance too: with Vienna in his hands, Hitler had military and economic control of the mid-Danube basin. Finally, the *Anschluss* encouraged the Sudeten Germans to campaign for their own inclusion in Germany.

Czechoslovakia and the Munich Crisis

It was this crisis that made Britain and France reluctantly face up to the fact that Hitler could not be appeased and that they must begin serious preparations for war. In the Peace of Paris, Czechoslovakia had been given territories – to improve its economy, transport, communications and ability to defend itself – to which it was not really entitled on the grounds of 'self-determination'. These territories contained large numbers of people of other nationalities: Poles, Hungarians, Ruthenes and, above all, over 3 million Germans in the Sudetenland areas. These minor nationalities, and the Slovaks, felt that the Czech-dominated government discriminated against them and, when the Great Depression added economic to political grievances, political disaffection grew. In 1936 the Sudeten German leader, Konrad Henlein, demanded autonomy for his people and the other national minority groups also began to demand concessions.

Hitler began his campaign to gain control of Czechoslovakia in late March 1938 as soon as he had achieved the *Anschluss*. He met Henlein and encouraged him to make increasingly extreme demands to which he believed the Czech government could not give way. Czech refusal led to false rumours on 20–21 May of an imminent German attack on Czechoslovakia. France (in keeping with its mutual defence agreement with Czechoslovakia), Britain and (separately) Russia warned Hitler against it and he hurriedly denied any intention of attacking the Czechs. A week later, however, he did issue the directive '*Fall Grün*' ('Operation Green') to prepare for the invasion of Czechoslovakia by 1 October.

Through the summer, Britain and France mediated between Germany and Czechoslovakia, trying to get Hitler to moderate his demands and the Czechs to agree to surrender the Sudetenland to him. By the beginning of September, he was making public threats of war against Czechoslovakia and demanding self-determination for the Sudeten Germans. There has been a lot of argument among historians about whether Hitler really intended to attack Czechoslovakia or whether he was just raising the pressure, having calculated that Britain and France were so weak-willed that they would crack under it sooner or later. Perhaps it doesn't much matter: the important point is that the attempts to buy him off by letting him have the Sudetenland were doomed to failure because that was not what he really wanted. The Sudeten Germans were just the excuse to pick the quarrel with Czechoslovakia which would allow him to swallow the whole country into his growing German Empire.

On 12 September, Hitler returned to the theme of the rights of the Sudeten Germans in a speech which prompted Neville Chamberlain to fly to Germany and speak to Hitler at Berchtesgaden. There, Hitler demanded that the Sudetenland be given to Germany. Chamberlain consulted the French government and they decided to offer Hitler all the areas where Germans were in a clear majority. Hitler rejected this and, at this point, Britain and France decided to support Czech resistance for which its army was mobilising. But then Chamberlain, supported by Mussolini, called for an international conference. Hitler agreed and it met at Munich on 29 September. Because Hitler and Mussolini had consulted beforehand over what Hitler was prepared to accept, they were able to get the British and French (Edouard Daladier) leaders to agree to what they had previously refused: areas with German majorities would be evacuated by 10 October and plebiscites held under international supervision in other areas. On their return from Munich, the three non-German leaders were apparently hailed by their relieved peoples as peace-makers.

More recent research suggests, however, that the public enthusiasm seen on the cinema newsreels in Britain, at least, was the result of a successful campaign to manage the news media by Chamberlain and his colleagues in the government. Several left-wing daily newspapers and the *Daily Telegraph*, which normally supported the government, called for Chamberlain to take a tougher stand against Germany.

British public opinion was probably already divided over the issue of whether to go to the Czechs' rescue before the Munich conference and then re-united against appeasement after it. Certainly, Hitler's unscrupulous and aggressive behaviour towards Czechoslovakia angered the British and French publics, as well as damaging Mussolini's reputation with the Italians. Hitler encouraged further unrest among the Slovaks and, when the Czech government moved to put it down in March 1939, used this as the excuse he had all the time been looking for to march German troops into Czechoslovakia and swallow it up.

Poland and the Nazi–Soviet Pact

As soon as the Munich Crisis was over, Hitler started to put pressure on Poland. He demanded the construction of a German road and railway across the Vistula corridor and that Danzig be returned to Germany. This time Britain and France were determined to give firm guarantees to all those countries they believed to be at risk of a German or Italian invasion. Immediately the German forces had occupied Czechoslovakia, they promised support in resisting German aggression to Holland, Belgium and Switzerland, followed by Poland, Greece and Romania.

Hitler did take the threats more seriously but believed that the system of alliances he had built up would prevent Britain and France giving effective support to Poland. In May, the Rome–Berlin Axis was turned into a full political and military alliance: 'The Pact of Steel'. In spite of the seizure of Memel from Lithuania, Hitler was also able to announce alliances with it plus Latvia and Estonia. Thus the Baltic states could not become an Allied base for aid to Poland

All now seemed to hinge on Stalin. He was entitled to feel bitter at having been excluded from the Munich Conference in spite of the fact that Russia had treaty commitments to Czechoslovakia and had offered help. There was also the problem that the Poles were extremely nervous about allowing Russian troops onto their soil and on all previous occasions had refused to consider it. Finally, there were doubts about the quality of the Red Army in the wake of Stalin's massive purge of its officers in 1937. Nevertheless, Russia was the only country which had the ability to offer immediate aid to Poland. Still France and Britain were unhappy negotiating with the Communist dictator and hesitated. Stalin seems to have concluded that they intended to desert him and the best he could do was to make a deal with Hitler, partly to allow Russia more time to prepare its own defence, in view of Hitler's stated ambition of achieving *lebensraum* at its expense. Thus on 24 August Hitler and Stalin made the Nazi–Soviet Non-Aggression Pact in which they cynically divided up eastern Europe between them. There was now no risk for Germany of a repetition of 1914 with a war on two fronts, and perhaps the Allies might not intervene at all. Thus the attack on Poland came on 1 September 1939. This time, however, Britain and France kept their word and declared war on Germany on 3 September. This, of course, was the start of the war in Europe but war in the Pacific followed in 1941.

Conclusion

The answer to the question 'When did the Second World War become inevitable?' should have emerged from the narrative. It was when Hitler's ambitions stretched beyond what Britain and France together were prepared to allow. As long as politicians and people could delude themselves into thinking that Hitler could be appeased, at the same time as being short of the necessary military resources to prevent him, war would not come. Once Hitler was seen as having unreasonable and even, perhaps, unlimited ambitions, then the mood of the people changed and, when Chamberlain proved unable to change, they changed their leader too. It may seem odd that they finally chose to take a stand over Poland, which they had no more chance of saving than Czechoslovakia. But it was the change of mood over the Czechs' fate that made people face up to reality – and having faced up to it, strategic considerations played little part in the decision to stand behind Poland. Who could know when, or if, a better moment to draw a line in the sand would present itself?

Examination essays on change and continuity

The big challenge with this type of question – which has a strong chronological element to it – is to avoid simply writing a narrative account (or 'telling the story'). Instead you need to produce a structured, analytical account in about 45 minutes. The trick is to look for the issues, rather than to think in chronological terms. Here are a couple of examples.

Change essay

When and why did the British Government abandon its policy of appeasement?

Begin by looking at the title for clues about how to structure the essay. The use of the two interrogative (questioning) words 'when' and 'why' gives away that this essay needs to have at least two main sections. The 'why' in this question also implies a third section, however – if the policy was followed and then abandoned, there must have been reasons for it which, at some point, become either irrelevant or less important than other factors. Thus this essay could have three sections:

1 Why did the government follow the policy of appeasement?
2 When was it abandoned?
3 Why was it abandoned (*i.e.* which of the reasons you have given in section 1 had changed and how)?

For section 1 refer back to chapter 3 (pages 60–1), for the reasons for appeasement, listed as A to F. Briefly explain them. For section 2 use this chapter (pages 119–20) to explain how the Czech crisis changed the opinions of both public and government in Britain. For section 3 look again at the six reasons you gave for appeasement in section 1 of the essay and point out the significant changes in A, B (chapter 2), C, E and F (chapter 4) in particular.

Write a conclusion about which were the crucial changes, and why.

This kind of structure will make it hard simply to narrate the story.

Continuity essay

How much continuity was there between the foreign policies of the Weimar Republic and Nazi Germany?

Again, in this slightly simpler essay, begin by looking for the issues, rather than fall into the trap of writing all about the Weimar Republic's policies first and then writing about Hitler's. So, what were the Weimar Republic's aims in foreign affairs and how do they match up to Hitler's?

	Weimar Republic	**Nazi Germany**
1	Reparations – successful	
2	Avoiding disarmament and commencing rearmament	Continuing and increasing rearmament
3	The *Anschluss* with Austria	The *Anschluss* with Austria
4	Joined League of Nations	Left League of Nations
5	Reluctant acceptance of Versailles losses of land	Regaining territory lost at Versailles and going on to ...
6		Conquest of *lebensraum*
7		Restoration of German pride
8		European domination
9		World domination?

In the essay, deal with the *issues* one at a time, then it is easier to point out when Hitler begins to diverge from, and go beyond, earlier German politicians.

FURTHER READING

There are many books on this period of history. There is room for only a fraction of them to be mentioned here – and many excellent ones therefore will not. Those listed are some that are helpful in particular ways.

General texts and chronological accounts

Robert Wolfson *Years of Change: European History 1890–1945* (Edward Arnold, 1978, revised edition) – written for A-Level students, good for getting a clear chronological outline.

David Williamson *War and Peace: International Relations 1914–1945* (Hodder and Stoughton, 1994) – a more recent chronological approach, with analysis.

Ruth Henig *Versailles and After 1919–33* (Methuen, 1984); *The Origins of the Second World War 1933–9* (Methuen, 1985) – both books, in the Lancaster Pamphlets series, are good, sharp analytical accounts; a bit more difficult to follow.

Martin Kitchen *Europe between the Wars* (Addison Wesley Longman, 1988) – good for extra factual information.

Books on specific aspects

R. M. Watt *The Kings Depart* (Weidenfeld and Nicolson, 1968). This is quite elderly now, but if you want to understand the atmosphere and context in which the Peace of Paris was made, there is no better book. But be warned – it is huge!

P. H. H. Bell *Origins of the Second World War in Europe* (Addison Wesley Longman, 1986) – has chapters on the economic, strategic and military aspects, as well as the events that led to war.

A. J. P. Taylor *The Origins of the Second World War* (Hamish Hamilton, 1961). The book that started the controversy. Remember to read this with care – Taylor is a very persuasive writer but many of his arguments have been discredited.

Three books that look back over the debate:

Gordon Martel (editor) *The Origins of the Second World War Reconsidered* (Unwin Hyman, 1986). Chapter 5 by Norman Rich deals with Hitler's foreign policy.

J. Hiden and J. Farquharson *Explaining Hitler's Germany* (second edition, Batsford, 1989). Chapter 5 is a good summary of the historiographical debate over Hitler's foreign policy.

Ian Kershaw *The Nazi dictatorship* (second edition, Edward Arnold, 1989). Chapter 6 does the same as Chapter 5 in this book.

For Hitler's economic policy and its relevance to his preparations for war see Richard Overy *The Nazi Economic Recovery* (Cambridge University Press, second edition, 1996).

The quarterly journal, *Modern History Review*, is produced for A-Level history students. Its articles are readable, up-to-the-minute and there is nearly always one on some aspect of this period.

INDEX

Longman History in Depth

Series editor: Christopher Culpin

Titles in the series

Hitler and Nazism (0 582 29736 2)

Causes of the Second World War (0 582 29650 1)

Stalin and the Soviet Union (0 582 29733 8)

The Russian Revolution (0 582 29731 1)

Parnell and the Irish Question (0 582 29628 5)

Gladstone (0 582 29521 1)

Chartism (0 582 29735 4)

Oliver Cromwell (0 582 29734 6)

Charles I (0 582 29732 X)

Henry VII (0 582 29691 9)

Addison Wesley Longman Limited,
Edinburgh Gate, Harlow,
Essex, CM20 2JE, England
and Associated Companies throughout the world.

First published 1998
© Addison Wesley Longman Limited 1998

Set in 9.5/13pt Stone Serif
Produced by Longman Singapore Publisher Pte Ltd
Printed in Singapore

ISBN 0 582 29650 1

Acknowledgements

We are grateful to Hodder & Stoughton Educational for permission to reproduce an extract
from 'The Hossbach Protocol' by Adolf Hitler, translated by G. Rayner in *The Great Dictators* .

We are grateful to the following for permission to reproduce photographs and other copyright
material:

AKG London, pages 13 above, 14 below; Will Dyson, *Daily Herald*, 13.5.1919 (Centre for the
Study of Cartoons & Caricature, University of Kent, Canterbury), page 17; Getty Images, page
13 below; Popperfoto, pages 13 centre, 15; David Low, *Evening Standard*, 4.10.1935. © Solo
Syndication (Centre for the Study of Cartoons & Caricature, University of Kent, Canterbury),
page 114; Topham Picturepoint, page 14 above.

Cover photograph: Demonstration in Trafalgar Square by unemployed at the beginning of
1939. Popperfoto.

The publisher's policy is to use paper manufactured from sustainable forests.